WELCOME TO
MY JUNGLE

AN UNAUTHORIZED ACCOUNT
of How a Regular Guy Like Me
Survived Years of Touring
with Guns N' Roses, Pet Wallabies,
Crazed Groupies, Axl Rose's
Moth Extermination System,
and Other Perils on the Road
with One of the Greatest
Rock Bands of All Time

WELCOME TO MY JUNGLE

By Craig Duswalt

BenBella
BENBELLA BOOKS, INC.
Dallas, TX

BenBella Books, Inc.
10440 N. Central Expressway, Suite 800
Dallas, TX 75231
www.benbellabooks.com
Send feedback to feedback@benbellabooks.com

Printed in the United States of America
10 9 8 7 6 5 4 3 2 1

ISBN 978-1-63774-431-4 (trade paper)

The Library of Congress has cataloged the hardcover edition as follows:
Duswalt, Craig.
    Welcome to my jungle : an unauthorized account of how a regular guy like me survived years of touring with Guns n' Roses, pet wallabies, crazed groupies, Axl Rose's moth extermination system, and other perils on the road with one of the great rock bands of all time / by Craig Duswalt.
        pages cm
    Includes bibliographical references and index.
        ISBN 978-1-939529-80-0 (trade cloth : alk. paper)—ISBN 978-1-939529-81-7 (electronic) 1. Guns n' Roses (Musical group) 2. Duswalt, Craig. 3. Concert agents—United States—Biography. 4. Concert tours—Anecdotes. 5. Rock musicians—Anecdotes. I. Title.

    ML421.G86D87 2014
    782.42166092—dc23
    [B]
                                        2013039791

Editing by Gary Peterson
Copyediting by Eric Wechter
Proofreading by Michael Fedison and Greg Teague
Cover design by Joe Potter
Text design by John Reinhardt Book Design
Text composition by Integra Software Services Pvt. Ltd

Special discounts for bulk sales are available.
Please contact bulkorders@benbellabooks.com.

For Natasha, Tyler, Ryan, and Hayden.

CONTENTS

STARS 159

QUICK STORIES, STATS, & FACTS   189

INTRODUCTION

FROM 1991 to 1994, there was no rock band on the planet bigger than Guns N' Roses. Their *Use Your Illusion* albums sold more than 14 million copies altogether. Singles such as "Welcome to the Jungle," "Sweet Child O' Mine," "Paradise City," and "November Rain" topped the charts. Tour dates sold out in minutes all over the world. Guns N' Roses was an unstoppable force—or so it seemed.

Unfortunately, the Use Your Illusion world tour would be the last for the band. When it ended, the "almost" original lineup would go their separate ways. To this day, the musicians who played on that tour have not performed together.

But what was it really like on the Use Your Illusion tour? How did it feel to be in the middle of one of the biggest events in the history of popular music? Some people may think they know what it's like because they saw the movie *Rock Star*. But the reality is very different. No one who wasn't there can really know what goes on behind the scenes during a rock concert.

But I know the reality, because I lived it.

As Axl Rose's personal assistant during the Use Your Illusion world tour, I saw weird stuff that would make your hair curl. I experienced things that would make most people run the other way and never look back. But I would never trade the experience for any amount of money.

Welcome to My Jungle is a collection of funny and interesting stories portraying what it's really like to live and work with a hugely popular rock band. I saw it all: the highlights, the lowlights, the good, the bad, and the just plain strange.

Readers of *Welcome to My Jungle* will be able to put themselves in the position of traveling with some of the most famous people in the world. I'm just a regular guy. I'm not a record industry mogul or even a professional musician. But in my position as Axl's personal assistant, I had unparalleled access to events and situations that no one has ever talked about before. Some of them might sound unbelievable, but they are true—I lived through them.

So many people wonder about what it would be like to witness history. What if you could have traveled at the right hand of one of rock music's most iconic, polarizing, controversial figures? What if you could have been there as he interacted with other legends, like Liz Taylor, Brian May of Queen, or Bono of U2? What if you could have seen all the crazy things that happen to famous celebrities on the road? What if you lived with a group of guys who seemed to have everything, but couldn't hold it together? *Welcome to My Jungle* will show you all these things from an insider's perspective.

Welcome to My Jungle is more than just insider stories about Guns N' Roses. It's also a look at the lifestyle of very wealthy, very famous people. It's a "regular guy" look at the kind of world that most normal human beings will never experience. It's difficult to even imagine the kinds of things that happen to megastars on the road. Some are good, some not so good.

Welcome to My Jungle is my account of what it's really like to live in the middle of a rock-and-roll hurricane, and walk out of it alive. Most of the conversations you will read are paraphrased, and, again, this is my version of what happened. I'm sure there are slightly different versions, and I might have mixed up a story with another story, and a city with another city, but this is what I remember from more than twenty years ago.

The legions of Guns N' Roses fans out there will love it, and so will anyone who wants an insider's view of what life at the top of the music industry is actually like.

So turn the page, and get ready for a wild ride.

WHO IS CRAIG DUSWALT?

"WHO IS CRAIG DUSWALT?" is one of the most frequently asked questions on a very popular Guns N' Roses website. Short answer? I was Axl Rose's personal assistant on one of the biggest tours in the history of rock n' roll.

Long answer? Read the book.

At the end of the *Making of Estranged* documentary, Axl decided to leave in a clip of me joking around with August Jakobsson, the documentary cameraman. On camera, I said, "I, Craig Duswalt, am responsible for Guns N' Roses. Me, Craig Duswalt. I did everything. Everyone else is nothing." Axl thought it was hysterical, so he decided to add it to the documentary. The rest is history. Now, GNR fans want to know who the hell Craig Duswalt is.

Some stories I tell in this book, you may have heard. Most you haven't. This book is my perception of what happened—and I was usually much closer to the event than anyone else, meaning my versions are probably the closest to the truth. I do understand there are two sides to every story. But this is MY truth.

I wrote this book because every time I tell someone I was Axl's personal assistant, I suddenly have their full attention. They always want to know something interesting that happened on the road. I usually share a couple of funny stories, but I always leave them wanting more.

To this day, I still get calls to do interviews. I turn down 99 percent of them. A few years ago, I answered ten questions via e-mail for an old, popular website called splat.com. Within two days, my interview was on more than 5,000 websites worldwide. It was incredible! It just goes to show that the fan base for GNR is still huge.

I consider the members of Guns N' Roses, and members of the GNR crew, my friends. That means this book will not reveal any really dark or destructive secrets—and I have hundreds. If you want those stories, you'll have to get me really drunk. Unfortunately for you, I don't drink anymore—partly because of my days on the road with Guns N' Roses.

A little backstory—I had previously toured with Air Supply as a band assistant. I took care of the band and the backstage area. I was basically the personal assistant to the entire band. This was my inauguration into the world of rock n' roll. It was quite amazing for a twenty-one-year-old kid straight out of college.

One of my "jobs" for Air Supply was to invite beautiful women backstage to keep up the image of a rock band having lots of women around at all times. The great thing about Air Supply was that they attracted about 85 percent women to their shows. Not that they would do anything with these girls—heck, most of them were married. But that's another book for another time. Anyway, I would hand out the backstage passes to these beautiful women so they could meet the band. One of the requirements for getting backstage was that they had to wear the pass on their shirt over their left breast. Sometimes the women asked me to put the backstage pass on for them. And so I did. (Hey, I was twenty-one—give me a break! You would've done the same thing.) I did make double sure I had their permission first. Air Supply was very popular at the time.

I grew up a lot traveling with Air Supply.

A few years after ending my stint with Air Supply I had an opportunity to tour with Guns N' Roses. I decide to take the plunge.

I found out very early that GNR was all business. Really. Okay, it was *mostly* business. However, we did manage to have some fun and interesting things happened to us on the road.

I joined the tour in November 1991—the month Freddie Mercury of Queen lost his battle with AIDS. I was, and still am, a huge fan of Freddie Mercury and Queen. I found out right away that Axl also loved Freddie. Because of Guns N' Roses I was lucky enough to meet hundreds of celebrities and rock stars. The only one I wished I could have met, but didn't get to, was Freddie Mercury.

A lot of wonderful things happened to me on the road. But the best was meeting my wife, Natasha. (No, she wasn't a groupie.) One of the best stories in this book is how we met.

I'm telling these stories because they are a part of rock-and-roll history. And I want to share them with everyone. I hope you enjoy!

Me, just before going on tour with Air Supply.

Author's Note

THERE WERE NUMEROUS PEOPLE involved in the Guns N' Roses World Tour, and obviously, there are many sides to every story. This book is filled with my versions of what happened in the stories I tell. They may vary from other versions, but this is what I perceived, and this is what I remember over twenty years later. As my buddy Duff McKagan said in his book, this is my truth.

HOW THIS ALL STARTED

HOW I GOT INTO THE "BUSINESS"

I had toured with Air Supply for about six
years (two of those years with Doug Goldstein,
who would later become the manager for
Guns N' Roses). But I was pretty damn lucky
to get in with Air Supply. In fact, I never even
had to fill out an application!

It was July 1983. I had just graduated col-
lege—State University of New York at Oswego. I was a business
major with a theater minor, but I was very involved in theater. I
had starred in numerous college productions in my junior and
senior years. Acting is in my blood forever.

My first job out of college was at the Westbury Music Fair
in Long Island. Westbury Music Fair was a 3,000-seat, in-the-
round venue that housed plays and intimate concerts. I was a
backstage runner, a gopher, the bottom man on the totem pole.
When acts came into town, I would pick them up at the airport.
Or I would pick them up at their hotel, and bring them to the gig

1

for sound check. And I always had to make sure they had what they needed backstage.

I only held this job for about a month, because I was about to meet someone who would change my life.

One of the shows that came to Westbury while I was there was the well-known musical *The Sound of Music*. It starred theater veterans Theodore Bikel and Roberta Peters. Once again, I was in charge of making sure all the actors had what they needed. To my surprise, the producers needed something a little different than the usual water or coffee. They needed a couple of actors to plays bit parts. I was chosen to play one of the Nazi soldiers.

In between getting shoe polish and kiwi slices for the cast, I was so happy to be "acting" in an Equity (professional) play. Granted, I was a glorified extra, but I was on the stage with Theodore Bikel and Roberta Peters! I became pretty close to some members of the cast during the two-week run. It was a great experience, but nothing close to what was about to happen.

The Australian pop band Air Supply came to the Westbury Music Fair to do two shows—one on Friday night and one on Saturday night.

What I did not know at the time was that Air Supply had just fired their band assistant because of excessive drug use.

I worked the show on Friday night, getting drinks, supplying towels, and so on. I met the two lead members of the band, Russell Hitchcock and Graham Russell, as well as their security guard, Bob Street. Nothing special, just "Hi!" and some small talk. But I was working my ass off that night, running around for everyone—but always with a smile and a positive attitude.

The next day I found out my mom and her friend had tickets to see Air Supply that night. I wasn't supposed to work that night but because my mom was going I asked my boss if I could come in again to work the second show.

Two weeks earlier, out of nowhere, knowing that Air Supply was coming to town, my mom said to me, "What if they ask you to go on tour with them, would you go?"

I said, "Who?"

"Air Supply, what if they ask you to tour with them?"

I said to my mom, "And why would they do that? You're crazy! Where do you come up with this stuff?"

I never gave it another thought.

I arrived at work about 2 p.m. to help get things ready for the Saturday-night show. At about 5 p.m., Air Supply arrived to do a sound check. Once again, there were casual hellos from the band members. But Bob Street talked to me a little about my interests, and how I liked working at Westbury. About a half hour later Bob and the band went back to the hotel to rest before the show, which was sold out.

As I got the backstage area ready, the excited crowd took their seats. About an hour later the warm-up band took the stage. I peeked out from behind the backstage curtain, and saw my mom and her friend in the audience.

Air Supply arrived through the Stage Door entrance. As the band members went to their dressing rooms, Bob Street pulled me aside and asked me how much I made working at Westbury. I told him about $150 a week. (Don't laugh. Back in 1983, $150 a week wasn't bad.)

Bob said, "How would you like to quadruple that?"

So many things went through my mind at that moment, one of them being, "What the hell does he want me to do to make $600 a week?"

My mind went to some very dark places. But I was twenty-one—and I was thinking to myself, *Hell, whatever he says, I'll do it.* I wouldn't really, but that's what I was thinking.

So I said, "Hell yeah . . . doing what?"

I was told that they needed a person to take care of their backstage area while they were on the road. They liked the way I worked the day before, so they wanted to offer me a job to join them on their world tour.

I was in shock. I think I said, "When do I leave?"

Bob said, "Come to our hotel tomorrow to iron out the details with our tour manager, John Slattery."

We shook hands and he went into a dressing room. I stood there dumbfounded, wondering what the hell just happened. Did I just get a job touring with one of the biggest pop bands around?

You bet your sweet ass I did. I would be leaving on Monday for a world tour with Air Supply, one of the most successful bands of the 1980s. And then I realized what my mom had said to me two weeks ago.

Holy crap—my mom's a psychic!

I was busting to tell the world what just happened. When the warm-up band finished I very coolly walked over to where my mom and her friend were sitting in the audience.

I casually said to my mom, "Do you remember what you asked me two weeks ago?"

She did not recall. (There goes the "my mom's a psychic" theory.)

"About touring with Air Supply," I reminded her.

"Oh yeah."

"Well, as crazy as this sounds, you were right."

"What are you talking about?"

"They asked me to tour with them. I leave on Monday."

At first my mom let out a small squeal, so as to not freak out or scare the other 3,000 people in the theater. But then she whispered to me, "Are they gay?"

Not a politically correct statement now, but in 1983 . . . Plus, she's a mom, and she was just concerned for her son.

(Let me set the record straight. Contrary to some beliefs, most of the members of Air Supply in 1983 were not gay. The only gay member of the band was their very talented keyboard player, Frank Esler-Smith. Frank became a very good friend of mine over the years, and it was a very sad day for me when Frank passed away from AIDS-related causes in 1995.)

My mom finally regained her composure.

As I left her to return backstage, I heard another squeal.

Again, it was her.

I just lowered my head and rushed behind the backstage curtain.

The next day I came back to the band's hotel and met with John Slattery, and I was "officially" hired on the spot.

That night I called all my friends from Deer Park, New York, and I threw my own last-minute going-away party.

The band sent a limo to my house the next morning, and it took me to JFK Airport. I hopped on a flight to Wallingford, Connecticut, checked into the hotel, rode with the band to the venue, and watched them take the stage.

As I watched the concert from the side of the stage, I just remember thinking to myself, *Wow! Damn! This is going to be very, very cool.* And it was.

I toured with Air Supply for six amazing years. They all remain great friends of mine to this day.

A side note: In 2006, I was on the Board of Advisors for the Michael Hoefflin Foundation, a Santa Clarita, California, charity that helps families with children who are diagnosed with cancer. The foundation asked me if I could get a band for their big fund-raiser. Twenty years after I toured with them, I asked Graham and Russell, and their manager, Barry Siegal, if they would do me a favor and perform for this charity. They didn't ask any questions—they were happy to do it. (They put on an awesome show!)

I owe most of my success to Russell Hitchcock, Graham Russell, Bob Street, and Doug Goldstein. Thank you, guys!

W

In between working for Air Supply and Guns N' Roses, I was employed as a waiter at Robaire's French Restaurant in Los Angeles. I was trying to make it as an actor, and the typical job for most actors in Los Angeles is being a waiter simply because it gives actors time to go on auditions during the day while waiting on tables at night. It was a very flexible job with very flexible hours.

One night, while working my station in the main dining room, a gentleman at one of my tables asked me to come over. He introduced himself as Hamilton Farmer, a psychic that had appeared on talk shows, including *The Tonight Show with Johnny Carson*.

"I don't usually do this, but because the feeling is so strong I felt I had to tell you something," Hamilton said.

For a moment it felt like he was trying to pick me up. Last time something like that happened I was a waiter at the Hamburger Hamlet Restaurant on Sunset Boulevard, also in Los Angeles. Another gentleman, Herbert Kenwith, a director for successful television shows such as *Good Times*, had asked me if I was an actor, and I said yes, and ten minutes later I had an audition the next day for the soap opera *General Hospital*.

He also asked me out to dinner.

I quickly told him, in a very nice way, that I wasn't interested in anything else, except maybe auditioning for *General Hospital*.

He understood.

And then he said, "Be at Gower Studios at 10 a.m. They'll be expecting you."

Now this stuff doesn't happen every day, but I've always believed you often meet people for a reason.

So because I still really didn't believe him, the next day I called the show and asked if I indeed had an audition. They said yes. I hung up the phone and raced over to Gower Studios, read for the *General Hospital* casting director, and got cast on the show as a waiter in Duke's Club. Typecasting? Maybe.

So I looked back at Hamilton Farmer.

"Tell me what?" I asked.

He explained again his extensive television resume and said, "You're probably an actor, right?"

"How'd you guess? You must be a psychic," I said sarcastically. Again, all waiters are actors.

He smiled.

"You are going to be very well known. In fact, you are going to be famous someday, and it has something to do with the letter *w*."

I didn't know what to think. I wanted to believe him, but I don't really believe in the whole psychic thing. And as if that weren't enough, he added, "And, you will be bigger than Bruce Willis." As a young actor at the time, I thought to myself, "Damn, that would be really cool."

He had my full attention now.

We continued to talk for a while, all the time totally convinced that I would be very successful someday.

I kept asking him what the *w* was, and for him to try harder to see (psychically) what the *w* was. I guess that was too difficult, because he kept "seeing" only the letter *w*.

So over the years I thought about what the *w* might be. Was it the first letter of a word? That seemed to make the most sense.

The word "writer" came to mind right away. Maybe I was going to become a famous writer. I was already a part-time writer. Again, so is everyone else in Los Angeles.

I had recently won a screenwriting fellowship for a screenplay I wrote from the Chesterfield Film Company sponsored by Amblin Entertainment, Steven Spielberg's production company. But even though I came close to selling a screenplay or two numerous times, that never panned out.

Then I thought the *w* might be my new stage name—Williamson—and that meant I was going to be a famous actor. I had recently changed my last name from Duswalt to Williamson for a while because I thought Duswalt might be too hard to pronounce. Well, aside from a few stints on television, and numerous stage plays, that didn't pan out either.

And while I didn't really believe in psychic readings, over the years I kept thinking what that *w* was, and how that *w* would put me on the map.

But all these *w*'s were the first letter in words and names. And Hamilton Farmer had said from the beginning, that he saw only the letter *w* alone. So, I think I was continually trying to put a square peg in a circle.

And then one day it dawned on me, years after touring with Guns N' Roses. And though it seems obvious now, it never hit me before.

I am currently a professional speaker and author and creator of the RockStar System For Success—How to Achieve RockStar Status in Your Industry. I have become very successful in the seminar industry in a short period, and I truly feel it's because I speak from the heart and I have a great brand—RockStar.

I teach entrepreneurs and corporations how to think outside the box and market themselves and their businesses, all like a RockStar.

So I thought to myself, even though I toured with Air Supply for six-plus years, the band that really put me on the map in the music industry was Guns N' Roses. Because of my associations with GNR numerous doors were opened for me and I met tons of influential people. So, it had to have something to do with Guns

N' Roses. But there's no *w* in Guns N' Roses. And I worked specifically for Axl Rose—again no *w*.

But then I remembered. Axl Rose's full name is W. Axl Rose.

And there you have it. The letter *w*. And it is all by itself.

My association with W. Axl Rose and Guns N' Roses helped me start my RockStar brand, and it introduced me to very influential people, who remain in my life to this day.

So I guess Mr. Hamilton Farmer did in fact "see" the letter *w*. Alone.

Wow!

Now, I know I'm not even close to a household name, and I'm definitely not more famous than Bruce Willis, yet, but in the seminar industry I am very well known because of my RockStar brand. And right now that is more than good enough for my family and me. I personally don't want to get too famous. I've seen what happens to people that have become very famous—and I would not wish it on my worst enemy.

I'm very happy with my success, and I'm very happy that I can walk down the street without being recognized.

I'm also very happy that I finally think I know what Hamilton Farmer saw back in 1985.

SHOULD I STAY OR SHOULD I GO?

October 15, 1991, had started out like every other day of the past few months. I went to the local gym in Playa del Rey, California, to watch my girlfriend at the time—Kim Evenson, *Playboy* Playmate, September 1984—swim laps in a pool because I had nothing else to do. I was a starving actor making very little money, so watching Kim work out was the highlight of my day. Pretty sad.

My pager (cell phones in 1991 were brand-new at best) went off. I didn't recognize the number but I called it back from the pay phone (yes, there were still pay phones in 1991) near the outdoor pool. It was Doug Goldstein, the new manager of Guns N' Roses.

Doug and I had toured together for years with Air Supply in the mid-1980s and we became very good friends. It's funny, I was the one who showed Doug "the ins and outs" of touring and he became one of the most influential people in rock n' roll in the 1990s.

Anyway, Doug asked me if I was ready to go back on the road. Axl Rose needed a *second* personal assistant for the upcoming Use Your Illusion world tour. The words "second assistant" sort of confused me because I never knew that someone would need more than one assistant. How foolish of me. I found out quickly that one assistant was not enough for Axl Rose while on the road.

So, I look at Kim in her bathing suit while she's doing one of her "5,000" laps, and I weigh the situation. Stay in Playa del Rey and watch Kim swim, or go on the road with the hottest band in the world. Again. Come to the gym every day and watch Kim swim 5,000,000 laps or go on the road with Guns N' Roses as Axl Rose's "second" personal assistant, whatever the hell that meant.

Damn, I thought to myself. *Tough decision.*

But I knew what I had to do. And that was go on tour with the biggest band in the world at that time, and break up with Kim via a phone call from far, far away.

MY FIRST DAY WITH GUNS N' ROSES

Being Axl's second personal assistant was more like being Blake's first assistant. Blake Stanton was Axl's personal assistant at the time, but he was so busy he needed an assistant. So, at first, I was technically the assistant to the assistant. But I was really Axl's assistant because I was doing everything for him. When Blake left (see the Alone in Germany story), I became Axl's first assistant. Then I needed an assistant, who became Axl's second assistant, or my assistant. (I won't judge you if you need assistance understanding the whole assistant thing.)

My first day on the job, I walked into Axl's living room in the Hollywood Hills. Blake immediately tells me to go get Slash at the Oakwood apartments at the bottom of the hill.

No, "Hi!" Just, "Get Slash."

I was thinking to myself, "Don't you want me to fill out a W-4 first?" Blake was a man of very few words, because as I would realize very soon, he had a lot on his mind.

"He'll be standing in the parking lot wearing black," Blake said.

Go figure. Slash wearing black.

I was really excited because I had never met Slash and on my first day of work he was going to be in my car.

I got in my car and headed back down the hill.

I arrived at the Oakwood apartments and I pulled up to Slash who was standing by himself in the parking lot. He was wearing black. Without saying a word he got in my car.

Now, I understand that I wasn't a scary looking guy, but c'mon. Shouldn't he have at least asked who I was?

Slash got in and said, "Hey."

I said, "Hey," back. "I'm Craig."

"Nice to meet you. You work for Axl now?"

I proudly said, "Yup."

He just smiled. A rather haunting smile at that.

We shook hands and I drove him to Axl's house without either of us saying another word the entire ten-minute ride.

Slash and I would go on to become very good friends. Drinking buddies on the road. In fact my first introduction to Everclear was with Slash. Would love to write about what happened that night, but I really can't remember a thing.

When Slash and I got back to Axl's house, Blake was on the phone.

I heard him say, "Brian, Axl, and I might have a doctor out here that we think can help Freddie . . ."

At first I didn't think anything of it, but as the conversation went on I realized he was talking to Brian May, the lead guitarist of Queen—my favorite band of all time.

I thought, *How cool was that?* First Slash, then we're on the phone with Brian May? This is going to be awesome. And I still hadn't even been introduced to Axl.

Without going into detail of the very confidential phone call, Brian apparently said, "Thanks for the offer, but Freddie was at peace and was ready to move on."

A few minutes later Axl walked out of his bedroom wearing only a pair of shorts. He walked right past me and asked Blake, "What did he say?"

Blake told Axl the outcome of the call and Axl rolled his eyes.

Axl sat on the couch, lit up a cigarette, and said to me, "Hey. I'm Axl."

As if I didn't know.

I walked over to him and shook his hand. "I'm Craig. Very nice to meet you."

And we went to work.

No fireworks, no big celebration for me starting my new, very cool job. Just a regular workday in Axl's house in the Hollywood Hills. The big topic of the day was why did Izzy Stradlin quit Guns N' Roses a few weeks prior? And how are we going to get new guitarist Gilby Clarke up to speed, fast?

Freddie Mercury passed away a few days later.

I am probably one of the biggest Queen fans of all time. I don't collect a lot of Queen stuff but I know pretty much everything there is to know about Queen.

When Freddie Mercury passed away it was a very sad day for me. Axl felt the same way. He was also a huge Queen fan.

I had no idea what direction the next three years of my life would take, but I knew it was going to be very interesting.

I was right.

ALONE IN GERMANY

Somewhere in Germany, four months into my job with Guns N' Roses, I had to run to a local mall to pick up a few things for Axl while he was asleep. I was really tired because I had only had about two hours of sleep myself. That was typical.

In the Guns N' Roses world this is how it works. The band does a show. The show ends between midnight and two in the morning. That's because GNR always went onstage late, which we will discuss later. Then on most nights, Axl would hang out for about two hours after the show in his dressing room. Then Axl, Blake, Axl's bodyguard, Earl, and I would take the limo to a restaurant for some late-night snacks—actually, full-on meals.

Axl hardly ever looked for five-star restaurants. He was very happy with the local Denny's or IHOP, especially because they were often the only restaurants open at 4 a.m.

The three of us nonsingers, all larger in stature than Axl, would order one meal. For me it was usually breakfast. But Axl would order at least three meals from the menu. Chicken fried steak was one of his favorites. He was always so hungry after a show, and he could never decide what he wanted to eat, so he would order multiple items and pick from each plate.

When we arrived at one of these fine establishments, it was virtually empty. One disheveled waitress, one male cook with a hairnet, half asleep, and a manager reading the daily newspaper for probably the fifteenth time with a cup of coffee.

It was always interesting to see the looks on their faces when they saw who just got out of the stretch limo and walked into their little restaurant.

The manager would always sit us in the "nicest" booth and usually ask for an autograph. Axl obliged.

The waitress would take our order and fumble her words while explaining the "specials." We were fully aware that Denny's never had specials, but when Axl was there, the waitress always wanted to spend as much time as possible at our table. So she made up some specials.

Happened all the time.

A once empty restaurant would somehow fill with people within fifteen minutes. It only took one phone call from an employee for the word to get out. And in small towns across the world, news spreads quickly. And remember, this is long before everyone had social media on their cell phones.

For the most part Axl would allow people to take pictures and he'd sign autographs, as long as they knew to leave us alone when the food arrived.

It was my job to make sure that happened. They did leave us alone, but they would stare from far away. Earl stepped in if a fan became a problem.

We'd finish up and get back to our hotel between 5:30 and 6 a.m., and I would be exhausted. But Axl often wanted to talk. Everyone else went to their nice comfy beds, but Axl wanted to talk. And Axl wanted to talk . . . to me. No one else, usually. Just me!

I always tried to "act" tired, but it never worked. Guess that's why I never made it as an actor.

Let me make this clear. During the day I could listen to Axl for hours. He's a very caring, very interesting person, and, yes, totally misunderstood by the public. He's also one of my wife's favorite people to this day. And Natasha is very careful about who she lets into her life. Axl and Natasha had some great discussions as well. It's just that I was exhausted, but he was still filled with a ton of energy having just wowed an audience of 80,000 screaming fans. It's very hard to come down off that high.

So I would listen. Sometimes for hours. Then Axl would go to bed, and while he slept, I had about two hours before I had to get everything ready for the next day.

So, on that day in Germany I was shopping for Axl on less than two hours of sleep. When I got back to the hotel, I saw Blake getting into a taxi.

And he was carrying all of his luggage!

I calmly asked him, "Where are you going?"

"I quit!" he exclaimed.

"What do you mean, you quit? You can't quit."

"Dude, I can't take this crap anymore. I'm outta here."

And with that he got into the cab and drove away.

That was it. That fast. Just left. And we were in Germany. I wondered how the hell was he going to get a flight back. It was going to be one very expensive ticket.

"Holy crap," I said out loud.

My first thought was, *Who's going to break the news to Axl?* Then I thought, *Hey, I'm about to get a raise.*

I had only been on the job for fewer than five months, but I felt I had a handle on things. I had wanted to do some things differently for a while, and now I was going to get my chance.

I headed up to our floor, knocked on Doug Goldstein's room, and told him the news.

He hardly seemed surprised and actually said, "Looks like you're going to be the man now. Good luck with that."

And he smiled.

I must have looked frightened, because then he said, "You'll be fine."

I immediately said, "I get another assistant, right?"

"Yes."

"Phew."

"When we get back to the States."

"Cool."

It wasn't until later that night that I realized we still had a month and a half left in Europe, and I had to do all the "assistant" stuff now by myself.

We met with Axl a few hours later and he took the news quite well. Then Axl and I had a heart-to-heart meeting.

When Blake was in charge he was practically attached to Axl. He did a great job, but in my opinion, he was in Axl's space way too much. He would wake up in the morning and sit in Axl's living room and wait for him to wake up. Whether they were in Axl's home in Hollywood or in a hotel living room, Blake just sat there silent, unable to get any work done.

On tour, even on a day off, he never left the hotel and never really got to enjoy the tour because he always felt he had to be right next to Axl, just in case he needed something, or if something went wrong. Blake always sent me out to do the errands, so I actually saw the cities we were in.

Because I would be alone in Europe, without another assistant for the next forty-five days, things had to change. Plus, I believed that because Axl was an adult, if he needed something he could just come to my room and ask me.

I told Axl that. I said that I had a lot of work to do to get ready for each show and to get ready for each new city, and that if he needed something that I was right next door.

Not only was Axl "cool with that," I think he felt relieved that he was going to get his space back, and not have some guy sitting in his hotel living room, waiting.

On that day, I gained respect from Axl, and we became great friends. I pitched my case and he understood. Axl was suddenly in a better mood, shows were going great, and everyone was getting along.

Only wish it would have stayed that way for the next two years.

Axl's first assistant, Blake Stanton, and me after the last show of the tour.

CASH

When you're on the road with a touring band—actually, let me clarify—when you're on the road with a band as huge as Guns N' Roses, you make a pretty good salary. And get this—almost everything you'd need is either supplied for you, or paid for by someone in the band or in management, or even by one of the promoters. In the morning there was always food around somewhere, there was lunch at the gig, and for me dinner was either with Axl, or once again at the gig.

Axl was extremely generous. Whenever I ate with him, which was almost all the time, he paid for everything.

On top of all this I received $50 per diem. That's another $350 a week for expenses of which I had almost none. Unfortunately, I was a young kid at the time, and I wish now that I had put at least half of that money away.

I also had "float" money. This was the band's money, or in my case, Axl's money, that I used to pay for things that Axl or the band wanted. I submitted the receipts and got reimbursed. This was so the band members didn't have to carry cash around. It just looked more rock star–like when they walked into a store, said to the salesperson, "I'll take that," and left. I would then pay for the item and take it with me. Hopefully, I would then catch up to Axl at the next store before he purchased his next item.

And then there was the "extra" cash to "take care of situations," so that people (witnesses) kept quiet about certain "things."

I carried a lot of "extra" cash—a lot of it. Sometimes I needed it, and sometimes it would just sit for weeks, burning a hole in my pocket. But I always had it with me just in case.

TRAVEL

HOW WE TRAVELED

When I toured with Air Supply from 1983 to 1988 most of our traveling was on those cool rock star buses. These "diesel pushers" had a front suite with couches, television, a VCR player, dining table, kitchenette, microwave, refrigerator, and a bay that stored ice and plenty of beer. We slept in the nine bunks in the middle section of the bus. You pretty much had to be drunk, though, to actually fall asleep in these coffin-like bunks. The back suite of the bus had more couches, one that pulled out into a large bed, and another television. I personally loved traveling this way. It was very easy because we could usually leave whenever we wanted, and we didn't have to deal with airports. Plus, the bonus of having the bus in the parking lot, available for an inexpensive late-night snack, or even better, raging late-night party, was perfect.

Totally different with Guns N' Roses. The crew, which I'm guessing had more than one hundred employees, traveled in *really* cool rock star buses. I traveled with the band and the band's entourage, which was about thirty of us. Because everything was so fast-paced, we only traveled on airplanes and in limos.

About two hours before we were scheduled to leave, we had to pack our suitcases and leave them outside our hotel rooms. Members of our security team (the really big guys) would then come by and pick up our luggage and load it into a cargo van. They would then take the van to the airport and load our plane.

Ninety percent of the time we traveled on a private plane—the *MGM Grand*. This was luxury at its finest. The plane had about thirty-five first-class seats, some individual, and some in staterooms at the back of the plane. In the middle section was a long bar filled with drinks and tons of incredible appetizers and desserts. We drank and ate like kings.

Airports were generally a pain in the ass, but our entourage was treated like gold. We would get into the limo at the hotel, drive to the airport, and drive directly onto the tarmac at the foot of the stairs to board the plane. We very rarely had to go through the airport because it was usually a complete melee if we did.

I loved to fly and traveling with Guns N' Roses took flying to a whole new level. I had never had a fear of flying until I experienced hell on a GNR flight from Kansas City to Denver. We flew in a massive thunderstorm, and the plane was tossed around like a cheese omelet. We all thought for sure we were going to die that night. I actually wrote a note to Natasha, telling her how much I loved her, and that this was good-bye, and I held it tightly in my clenched fist until we landed safely. Axl sat very quietly next to his sister Amy the entire flight. It was eerily quiet the whole time. When we landed we heard that our pilots were even freaking out. To this day I hate flying, all because of that flight.

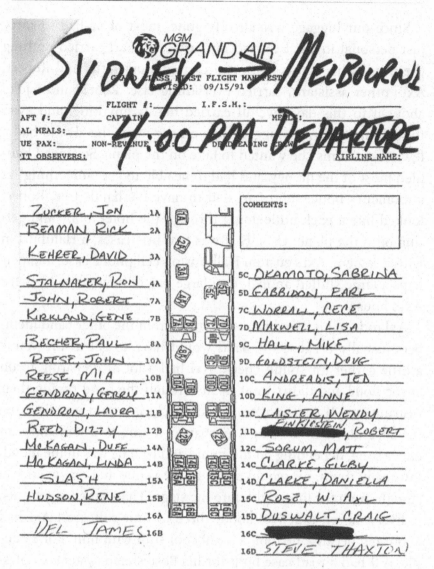

Typical seating chart on our private jet.

Since our luggage was already gone, most of us had to carry just personal items. I carried my briefcase, Earl carried nothing (he needed his hands free), Axl carried a cigarette, and Robert, Axl's other assistant, carried everything else. Robert and I joke about it to this day—we all carried hardly anything, and even though most of Axl's luggage was on the plane, he always had a few other "items" he wanted to take on the plane. So since I handled most of the money, and had to be able to get "something" at a moment's notice, and Earl had to have his hands free, Robert looked like a pack mule going through the hotel lobby and getting onto the plane. Usually it was two briefcases, a Halliburton with a camera, Axl's custom Halliburton cell phone case, and perhaps a large stuffed animal, or a large bag of new tchotchkes for Axl's house.

Axl rode in his own limousine, apart from the other band members, usually because the band would have to get to the venue a little earlier for sound check. Axl had a lot of preparing to do at the hotel and didn't want to sit through the band tuning their instruments. If Axl went to sound check, it would usually be at the tail end. He would sing a few bars of a song, and sometimes an entire song, depending on the sound and/or if he was in the mood. But many times, we would arrive at the venue and Axl would go straight from the limo right onto the stage. That's when it got nuts.

Everyone on tour had about three to four suitcases. Axl had about ten because he took a lot of cool stuff with him. For example, Axl had a road case built for his Bose stereo system. Coolest sound system I've ever heard.

Another one of Axl's extravagant items was a huge road case, about eight feet tall and about ten feet long, designed to hold his workout machine called the ROM exercise machine. I think you work out on this thing for three seconds a day and you have a six pack in about a week—something crazy like that. It's an amazing piece of equipment.

This monstrosity did not fit in his hotel room so the luggage guys always had to get "special permission" to set up outside of Axl's room on the floor we were all staying on. We needed numerous extension cords to reach my room and plug it in.

Axl worked out on his machine almost every day and all of us were welcomed to use it whenever we wanted. But for some reason we never did. Well, at least I know that I never did. I remember sitting on it once, but I also remember I was smoking a cigarette. I smoked three packs a day, and dipped Skoal at the same time. Plus, I was too busy, usually handling about 4,000 problems every hour, to even think about getting healthy. Just an excuse, I know.

DECOYS

Axl wanted to wear an Everlast robe and boxing gloves for the bow after every show. My buddy Denis Clancy from Long Island hooked me up with the Everlast robes and tons of boxing gloves.

So, at the end of every show Axl ran to his onstage dressing room and put on a red Everlast robe and a pair of Everlast boxing gloves, previously autographed by him before each show. He then ran back onstage for the bow, threw the boxing gloves into the crowd, and threw out dozens of red roses, as well.

He would then either run directly offstage and straight into a limo and we'd head back to the hotel or to the plane, or he would head back to his dressing room and hang backstage. But he was known for always wearing the red Everlast robe at the end of every show.

Enter the second red Everlast robe.

Fans often lined the streets outside the hotel to get a glimpse of the band. In the United States it was bad, but overseas, it was unbelievably insane. I wasn't even in the band, but if I was in public, and it got out that I was on tour with Axl Rose and Guns N' Roses, I had a hard time the rest of the day. Just walking to the limo going to or from a show we would get pulled and yanked at if there was a lapse in security. Fans ripped clothes, pulled hair, and tried to grab anything we were carrying. It was relentless. It was frenzied. And it was very dangerous for the star.

So, sometimes we set up decoys to disperse the fans and/or the paparazzi while we went where we needed to go. Sometimes it was someone from the crew or even someone working at the venue. I also had the "pleasure" of being a decoy a few times—one time because of what I will just call the "St. Louis situation" and leave it at that for legal reasons.

I was also used as a decoy to get the fans to think that Axl had left the backstage area immediately after the show so they wouldn't wait around. When the band left later on, they could leave in peace. So, immediately after the show, I put on the second red Everlast robe and a red Everlast hat. I ran straight into a limo and headed out from the backstage area. I left the window open and flashed a peace sign, and most people thought I was Axl. I think Ronnie also did this for Slash. Ronnie had the same exact haircut, and because the hair was usually covering Slash's face it was easy for Ronnie to be mistaken for Slash.

I used to love being a decoy, because it usually meant I got to be alone for a little while away from all the craziness.

I remember one specific time we used a limo as a decoy. The band and entourage went out to dinner one night at the River Café, a floating restaurant on the River Seine, in Paris, to celebrate GNR's manager, Doug Goldstein, and his wife, Jenny's, second wedding anniversary.

During the day hundreds of fans had gathered outside the Hôtel de Crillon and followed us to the restaurant. From inside the restaurant we arranged for a decoy limousine to go to the front entrance. Most of the fans were at the front door when the band made their escape unnoticed from a side entrance in a regular van. The rest of us "not-so-famous" people walked right out the front door and into the awaiting limo. Most fans realized that we weren't the band and that they had missed the band's exit, but believe it or not there were a few crazed fans that pursued our limo on a high-speed chase around the streets of Paris.

BATH SALTS

In one of Axl's suitcases we always had on hand about fifteen to twenty bags of special bath salts that weren't available in your typical bath and body store. I forget the purpose for the bath salts, except for the obvious use in a bath, but that doesn't matter for this story. What does matter is that they were kept in plastic baggies inside medium-sized gold boxes. Yes, they looked like bags of pure cocaine. And we were Guns N' Roses. Potentially, a very bad combination.

We were in Tel Aviv, Israel, and we had to get on a commercial flight, so that meant we had to go through the airport—the regular airport with the regular police. Robert was carrying one of Axl's Halliburton suitcases, and inside the suitcase are maybe three to four of these bags filled with the white-powdered substance in the gold boxes. We were in a hurry and he did his best pack mule impression. Axl, Earl, and I led the way, walking briskly through the airport so we didn't get stopped by a gaggle of fans.

Robert started to lag behind, and I could only assume it was because he was carrying numerous bags. I figured he'd catch up when we got to customs, so we pressed on.

A few moments later I looked behind, and I saw Robert slowing down. I took a closer look, and he seemed to be dragging his right leg, almost Igor-like from the Frankenstein movies.

Again, I thought nothing of it, because my focus was to get Axl on the plane with as little fan interference as possible.

We arrived at the customs line, and I looked back to see Robert, still dragging his feet, but now sweating. He finally arrived at the gate in a panic, stress written all over his face.

He whispered, "One of the bags broke."

I didn't follow.

He whispered again, "The bath salts," as he subtly points to the trail of white dust about fifty yards long. His attempt at covering up the powder was futile at best.

My immediate thought was that we were in a foreign country. I started thinking that customs would have a field day with him. Strip search came to mind.

But in all seriousness, this was bad. As I looked around the airport I saw that it was filled with soldiers carrying machine guns.

We opened the Halliburton suitcase and there was white powder all over the place. One of us was going to have to take one for the team because we could not get Axl involved with trying to explain that the powder was bath salt, so I did the manly thing and told Robert to deal with this while I made sure Axl got on the plane with no incident.

Robert frantically, and very carefully, fixed the leak in the bag before he had to go through customs to board the plane.

As Axl and I got through customs unscathed, I turned to see Robert going back over his trail, shuffling his two feet over the white powder trail, blending it into the carpet. It was quite the dance.

I kept thinking of the movie *Midnight Express* and thought that Robert might get to experience that. But God was shining on us that day because Robert made it through customs and onto the plane. Disaster averted.

But those damn bags of white powder almost came back to haunt us again in Buenos Aires, Argentina, on the last two days of the Use Your Illusion tour.

AUTOGRAPHS AT CUSTOMS

When we traveled abroad, between countries, we flew on the *MGM Grand*. And because the fan base overseas was absolutely crazy, airport personnel preferred that Guns N' Roses didn't stroll through their airports and go through customs the "regular" way. Most of the time the customs officers boarded the plane as soon as we arrived at the gate. They scanned the plane, did a quick head count, and stamped our passports.

Now, that's how to travel overseas.

But when we had to fly commercially to foreign countries, it became an epic pain in the ass.

Case in point.

Pretty much every time Axl went through customs he was detained. Robert and I were let through pretty easily. Earl, probably because he was so big and looked mean (although he's a teddy bear), got through easily as well. But Axl, the slightest built of all of us, with the least-threatening demeanor, got stopped pretty much all the time.

I've witnessed it—he didn't act like a pompous ass—in fact he was always on his best behavior, because he wanted to get through without being detained.

The customs officials not only asked him a million questions at their podium, but also they sometimes asked him to step aside and eventually brought him to "the room."

I never went with Axl into "the room," but I'm pretty sure he was never strip searched while I was on tour. But he was asked numerous questions about everything.

Here's the deal. They detained Axl, asked him tons of questions, and then started trying to be his friend.

Axl *hated* this.

To make matters worse, after they tried to joke around with him for about twenty minutes—with him playing along so it would go faster—they had the audacity to ask for his autograph.

This happened in London after the Freddie Mercury Tribute. I'm not sure if it was at customs (I'm pretty sure it was) or whether it was just a security guard who wanted to meet Axl, but they singled him out again, and after he was detained for a little while Axl released a press statement that went something like this: "Having just given what I consider to be the best performance I am capable of at this point in my career, I totally understand why someone in the UK would want to needlessly harass me in this way."

Axl continued, "I don't expect to be treated any differently from anyone else traveling in and out of Britain and I understand these people have a job to do. However, to be singled out by someone who just wants to score a few points and have a story to tell his friends over a beer is really out of order."

And that pretty much sums it up right there.

Don't get me wrong, fame has its perks. Amazing perks. But when it gets to the point where you can't eat at a restaurant without someone taking your picture while your mouth is full, where you can't go to a public event without everyone telling you how wonderful you are, and not letting you enjoy the event, and where you cannot travel without getting detained so they can tell their friends they met Axl Rose, it gets old very fast.

This is why you see rock stars in the news for "being bad" in public. There are days when they just want to be left alone, and it's not possible.

So when people tell me that they want to be famous I always say, be careful what you wish for, because you just might get it.

LIMO ACCIDENTS

One of the perks of traveling with Guns N' Roses was that we traveled in limousines pretty much all the time. Big limousines.

Another perk is that you get to travel the world. Between Air Supply and Guns N' Roses I have toured the world eight times. I've been on every continent except Antarctica, and to every state in the United States except Alaska.

Pretty cool for a normal kid from Deer Park, New York.

And sometimes you get to go to some really cool places. Places that you might not ever take your family on a vacation, but that you're so glad you're seeing—places like Prague, Czechoslovakia, which is an absolutely beautiful and interesting city. When we arrived there I thought to myself that I really wanted to see this beautiful city because I had a feeling I would never come back again. You see, we weren't exactly welcomed with open arms. We had to switch hotels because our original hotel found out we were Guns N' Roses, and not the John Reese Group, as noted on the reservation. Our booking agent always booked Guns N' Roses under our tour manager's name—the John Reese Group—for obvious reasons. When I went on trips with Axl, we always booked as the Craig Duswalt Group.

Most times, when the band arrived, it was the hotel staff who realized that we were Guns N' Roses. And they were very excited to see and meet the band. Plus, it's usually great publicity for a hotel to put up a famous band.

But not in Czechoslovakia. The hotel we booked did not want Guns N' Roses to stay in their hotel. I guess they heard the stories of trashed hotel rooms and flying television sets. Not that any of those things ever happened (while I was looking). But we finally got booked into another hotel and all was good.

Anyway, I got the chance to explore Prague because Axl was busy and didn't need me around for a few hours. I jumped on the opportunity. I called my buddy Kirt Klingerman, who worked as an assistant to Doug Goldstein, and asked him if he wanted to check out the city.

We met in the lobby and had every intention of taking a taxi around town. But as we walked out the front door of the hotel, we saw a few limos sitting in the driveway, each with a limo driver standing next to the car. Now Kirt and I knew there was no show that night, so we decided it would be okay to take one of the limos for ourselves.

We told the driver that we wanted to tour the city, and without questioning who we were he opened the back door for us and we jumped in. He spoke broken English and understood most of what we said. And we were off.

"That was easy," I said.

The driver pointed out some buildings of interest, and we took some really cool pictures. After about an hour or two of driving around and checking out some amazing places on foot, Kirt and I decided to head back to the hotel. All the while, every time we got out of the limo, people looked at us to try to figure out who we were. Obviously they never did, because we weren't anyone famous.

We jumped back into the limo and told the driver to take us back to the hotel. He seemed to slur his words a little as he confirmed our request.

And with that, he pulled out of his parking spot along the street curb, and slammed right into the back of a Czech police car.

I exclaimed, "Damn, he just hit a cop," stating the obvious.

The cop got out of his car, and walked over to our limo. He looked pissed.

Our limo driver said, "Stay here," and got out of the limo.

As if we were going anywhere. If we could've found a way to hide in the trunk we would have.

A discussion between our driver and the cop ensued, as we sat there trying to figure out how we're going to get back to the hotel if the driver got arrested.

We were freaking out. As a foreigner, the last thing you want is to be involved in an accident with a police officer. So many things could go wrong. After a few minutes the driver got back in the limo, and we took off.

I asked, "Is everything okay?"

The driver said, "Not really."

Kirt and I looked at each other, wondering if we were heading back to the hotel, or if the limo driver was instructed by the police officer to drive himself to the local jail and book himself. We made it back to the hotel, but over the next three days we never saw our driver. Maybe he really did get in trouble. But at least he got us back to our destination.

When I first started with Guns N' Roses, Axl, Earl, Blake, and I were in a limo coming home from a concert in Boston, and it was snowing really hard. It was about two or three in the morning. We also had two female passengers with us. Not sure how they got there, they just kind of appeared.

The highway was very icy and the limo driver, while being very careful, was going about 50 mph. Suddenly we started swerving. And from my college days in Oswego, I happen to know that swerving on ice, on a freeway, is not good.

The limo driver lost control of the very long stretch limo, and we slammed sideways into the center divider. All of us went flying in the back of the limo because we weren't wearing seat belts. But we weren't done yet—we were still moving.

Now I'm not an expert on accidents, although I have been in a few, but time kind of stops when you're in the middle of an accident.

We careened off the center divider, slid sideways back across the five lanes, and headed toward a ditch. What's weird is that it probably took about three seconds to slide across the highway, but it seemed like five minutes. I remember looking out the window and how long it seemed I was waiting for the next impact. But then we hit the ditch and slid down a small embankment, and once again we were thrown around the back of the limo.

We finally came to a sudden stop.

Everyone asked one another if they were okay. I had a major pain in my left rib area, because I flew across the seat into Blake's knee, but it was well worth it because one of the beautiful ladies landed face first into my lap.

I ended up breaking a rib and had to wear a sling for about two weeks. This was one way of not having to carry any extra luggage.

SHOTS FIRED: BOGOTÁ, COLOMBIA

On November 27, 1992, the day before my thirty-first birthday, we arrived in Bogotá, Colombia, from Venezuela. As we left Venezuela there apparently was a military coup and most of the stage equipment couldn't get out of the country. I look back on this now, and I thank God that we made it out safely, because we found out later that we were actually in a lot of immediate danger and never knew it.

GNR was scheduled to perform two very large shows at El Campin Stadium. But because we didn't have half of our equipment the production team had to decide whether to bring in new equipment from North America, or get their incarcerated cargo released from Venezuela. Both options were impossible for the first show on Saturday, so they decided to make Saturday tickets valid for Sunday and the two gigs were rolled into one. The band had wanted to play the second show on Monday, but because people had traveled long distances for the concerts, they felt that many couldn't stay the extra two days.

Natasha, who was my fiancée at the time, was on the road with us in South America. And what an interesting first few days she had. She arrived in Caracas, Venezuela, and I met her at the airport. Unfortunately her luggage wasn't there to greet me as well. Because we were on a tight schedule, she didn't have time to go shopping for new clothes, so she lived out of her carry-on for the first two days. Her luggage arrived just in time to come with us to our next stop in Bogotá.

We arrived safely in Bogotá. As is policy with GNR, wives and girlfriends usually traveled in their own limo or an SUV, or in the case of Bogotá, an old school bus. Not exactly the first-class ride they were used to. Natasha was the only wife/girlfriend on the road with us at this time, so she rode the bus with Sabrina Okamoto, Axl's masseuse, Amy, Axl's sister, and a few other members of the crew.

As usual, I rode in the limo in front of them with Axl, Robert, and Earl.

As we left the airport in our cavalcade I kept looking to see if the bus was still behind us because the driver looked very suspect. He was probably a great guy, but he was carrying my precious cargo.

We started driving through the city streets, and about ten minutes into the ride I didn't see the bus anymore.

I tried not to think anything of it. I was reasonably sure they were safe because we always had the highest security. But you just never know. And when I couldn't see anyone behind us I thought I was just being paranoid.

Well, I wasn't being paranoid. Something did go horribly wrong.

Our limo arrived at the hotel and I made sure Axl got up to his room safely, then I immediately headed back down to the lobby to wait for Natasha's arrival. About fifteen minutes later their bus pulled up to the hotel. *Phew*. But as the bus got closer I could see that it looked a little different than it had about thirty minutes before. It had shattered windows and holes.

I took a closer look and because I have seen *Godfather* movies and *Scarface*, I realized that these were bullet holes. I panicked.

Thankfully, almost immediately, Natasha and everybody else got off the bus, laughing and giggling. They told us that they were shot at as they rode through the city streets, and that they all had to "hit the deck" while bullets pelted the bus. But they were fine. They were laughing because they were freaking out so much, and it was so insane that they just had to laugh.

No one knew why they were shot at or where the bullets came from. They all said it was very surreal. To the driver's credit, he just kept driving, as if this was a common occurrence.

To say that they were shaken up is an understatement. Natasha and Sabrina were afraid the bus was going to stop, and if they weren't killed, they thought they would be sold as sex slaves.

But, we're all professionals, so we rose above it, and Guns N' Roses went on and performed on that Saturday night, and it was an amazing concert. The people of Bogotá were amazing. Just wish we knew why someone decided to shoot at our bus.

We laugh at it now, but it was far from funny back then.

THE SHOT HEARD AROUND THE HOTEL

All over Europe, fans are very passionate about their favorite bands—Guns N' Roses included. They get to concerts early, they stay late, they sing the words to every song (even in non-English-speaking countries), and they also love to grab. Grab at anything close to them—hair, clothes, body parts, and skin. Let me tell you, having your skin pulled in twenty different directions hurts.

Yes, even though I was not the rock star, I was used and bruised before, during, and after tons of shows. Most fans didn't care if I was a rock star or not. I worked for Axl, and that was good enough; or because I was always next to him, and they just grabbed for anything, I was collateral damage.

We had just finished a show in Modena, Italy, at Stadio Alberto Braglia, and the band members, excluding Axl, and their entourage, headed back to the hotel. Ninety percent of the time the band left the venue first. Axl left a couple of hours later, usually with me, Earl, Robert, and Steve, Axl's chiropractor. On this night Steve was lucky enough to have left earlier with the band.

Just as we sometimes used decoys to stand in for Axl, we also used decoy limos. When we left a concert we used two limos, one with Axl and us, and a much nicer limo with the driver by himself. We figured that people would assume Axl was in the nicer limo. Sometimes we took a van or a regular car back to the hotel while the beautiful limo in front of us had no one in it. It was worth the extra expense.

When the nice limo pulled up to the front door of the hotel, the fans attacked it thinking Axl was going to get out. While that melee took place we calmly had our driver take us around to the side door or the loading dock, and we walked into the hotel unscathed.

Sometimes we'd go to the lobby and watch the driver of the decoy limo in front of the hotel as he tried to convince thousands of people that Axl was not in his limo. Not a pretty sight, but very humorous.

This particular night there were hundreds of fans waiting for Axl to arrive back at the hotel after an amazing show. But because it was only about fifteen feet from the limo to the front door of the hotel lobby, we figured we would take our chances.

There were protocols we followed in these situations, and we took them very seriously. Unfortunately, Axl never listened to these protocols.

We pulled up to the hotel and because we're *really* smart, we told the driver to pull around to the side of the hotel so we could get out there after Earl "cleared" the area.

Earl is an ex-NFL player. He can clear an area.

We pulled up to the side of the hotel, and within seconds the hundreds of fans from the front of the hotel surrounded our limo. Europeans are very fast. Even Earl couldn't clear this area. We needed help.

At that point, "protocol" was for Earl to get on the walkie-talkie and summon help. Because the tour was very high security, we all carried walkie-talkies 24/7. If we needed help it would literally be there in seconds. This was very comforting and very helpful on numerous occasions. So we knew that as soon as Earl got on the walkie-talkie, within seconds, we would have the place cleared by our team of very large bodyguards with booming voices and we would calmly walk into the hotel, to our rooms, and straight to bed.

Didn't happen.

On this night, out of nowhere, as we sat in our safe limo, surrounded by hundreds of very "passionate" European fans, we heard the following come from Axl's mouth:

"I'm going for it."

Seemingly less than a millisecond later, Axl opened his door and leaped into the crowd.

With that, Earl, Robert, and I looked at one another in horror and yelled, "Damn!" as we jumped out of the limo to try to save Axl, who was engulfed in a sea of Guns N' Roses fans.

Imagine a slab of meat surrounded by thousands of piranha. You get the picture.

The biggest melee to date was taking place and it starred Axl Rose. Our job was to get him out of there, intact, and preferably with his clothes still on his body.

Earl threw people around, left and right, trying to get to Axl, and Robert and I pushed our way through as well. We were grabbed and scratched, but felt no pain because the adrenalin had kicked in.

To make matters worse, there were a lot of paparazzi in the melee as well, taking pictures of Axl fighting his way through the crowd. Axl does not like his picture taken.

So, because we knew that Earl would eventually get to Axl, Robert and I turned our attention on getting the paparazzi "out of the picture." Most paparazzi are exactly who they are portrayed to be in the news—ruthless, rude, disgusting human beings with no moral compass.

As soon as we decided to confront the paparazzi, Axl got plowed into by one of the camera-toting dirtbags and fell to the ground. Robert got in Mr. Dirtbag's face. Axl got up and got in Mr. Dirtbag's face.

Then the dirtbag shoved his camera in Robert's face, and Robert grabbed the camera and smashed it to the ground.

It was beautiful. Paparazzi boy was in total shock, shouting out what we assumed were Italian curse words. Funny, it was okay for him to plow into our lead singer, but as soon as we defended ourselves, he got upset. And I mean upset.

The frenzy to get a piece of Axl and his clothing had escalated into a full-fledged brawl with hundreds of people wailing at each other—friends hitting friends, brothers hitting brothers, moms hitting grandpas . . .

Suddenly, out of nowhere, a gunshot went off.

Everyone stopped.

Silence.

We all looked at each other.

Still.

And simultaneously we all started checking our bodies for a single gunshot wound. I felt around my chest, my arms, my legs, freaking out, because in my mind that bullet had to go somewhere, and at that moment, we were the enemy.

I looked around and everyone else was doing the same thing—checking to see if they were hit.

Then, like the parting of the Red Sea, people backed away to reveal an Italian policeman standing at the top of the stairs, seemingly in his own outdoor flood light provided by the hotel, with his gun held high up in the air, smoke coming out of the barrel.

It was like a movie.

The policeman came to save the day.

Axl and I looked at each other for a split-second and without saying anything, took the opportunity and darted into the hotel, untouched. Earl and Robert followed.

We were finally safe.

But we didn't go to bed . . . obviously.

We went straight to the bar and got lit, and told everyone the story how we all thought for one second that we were shot.

About an hour later the police arrived and they wanted Robert's passport. The dirtbag paparazzi guy wanted to press charges and the police were there to arrest Robert.

Now the Guns N' Roses band members and entourage were big on practical jokes, so Robert wasn't sure if this was real. But this time it was, and Robert explained later that he kept thinking about what can potentially happen in a foreign jail.

But it just so happened that our promoters and managers "know people" and the charges were dropped. Robert just had to pay for Mr. Dirtbag's new camera.

Axl paid for the guy's camera.

ALMOST MISSED MY FLIGHT

We had this thing on the road where if you were late, especially if you weren't a band member, they would try to leave you in the city you were in, and you would have to make it to the next city at your own expense.

Harsh.

Almost happened to me when I first started with Guns N' Roses in Oklahoma City, Oklahoma.

Axl had gone to see U2 with Doug, the band manager. So, I had the night off. And because I was single at the time, I went out on the town, and I met a lady friend. We had a few drinks. Okay, we had a lot of drinks—it was my night off.

A few hours later I took my lady friend to my hotel room, you know, just to talk about life.

After a while, there was a knock on my door.

"Let's go, Duswalt," someone shouted. It was obviously someone from the security team.

"Be right there."

Unfortunately we weren't finished talking.

About five minutes later we finished our conversation, and I rushed downstairs. I got to the front of the hotel and the cars were gone. I ran around the side of the hotel. Nothing. To the back of the hotel. Nothing.

Suddenly I realized what was happening. They were trying to leave without me. And worst part was it wouldn't even be their fault because they told me they were leaving. I was just late.

I thought to myself, *If i'm not on that plane, Axl is going to be pissed.*

I had already left my luggage outside my hotel room door an hour earlier, so that had been picked up. I had nothing. In fact, to make matters worse, my wallet was in my briefcase, and they took my briefcase as well.

I kept thinking what to do next, knowing that if I didn't make that flight I was screwed.

So I ran back up to my room, and luckily my lady friend was still there.

"You need to drive me to the airport," I pleaded.

She agreed.

We ran as fast as we could to the elevator, got down to the lobby, ran to her car in the parking lot, and raced toward the airport.

And get this . . . because we had been to so many places, and because I didn't have my briefcase, and because the itinerary was in my briefcase, I had no idea what city we were going to next. It could have been anywhere in the United States.

So I asked her to really speed it up. The cars had left about twenty-five minutes before we did, so I figured we could catch them. They still had to load the plane. Unfortunately, I knew what was happening—they were going as fast as humanly possible, because they wanted to leave someone behind. Again, they loved playing pranks.

We arrived at the airport, but there was another problem. Our plane was loading on the tarmac that night, so no one was going through the airport. The only cars allowed on the tarmac were the limos. Plus, even if I had clearance, I wouldn't have known where to begin looking for the gate or the opening where a car could get onto a tarmac.

I imagined the guys cracking up while loading the plane— loading the plane faster than it's ever been loaded.

We drove to where we could see the planes. It was a little off course but I figured our plane would be away from the normal area of the airport.

And there in the distance, way in the distance, I saw the *MGM Grand*. But there was a really tall security fence between it and me. But at least the plane was on the ground, so there was still hope.

We drove all around the perimeter of that fence, looking for any opening that would fit a car. I figured, even if I got in trouble for driving on the tarmac, the band would explain who I was, and they would let me go.

Maybe.

In the world we live in today that would not be possible, but in the early 90s, there was no TSA.

We continued to drive, and suddenly I saw two limos driving into the airport. *Could it be?* I thought. *We beat them here?*

I knew we had driven fast, but not that fast.

We raced over to the limos to cut them off.

Again I thought that I was so fortunate that Axl didn't see any of this. And Doug, he would not have appreciated my being late, and even worse, he didn't like when the members of the entourage drank, because we always had to be alert, just in case.

We pulled up to the limo, and I quickly thanked my lady friend, and hopped out of her car. I ran to the back passenger seat of the limo, opened the door, and jumped in.

Right onto Axl's lap.

I looked up and smiled, and gingerly took the unoccupied seat across from Axl. To make matters worse, there was Doug sitting next to Axl.

The cars that had taken the band and the entourage to the airport, the cars I was supposed to be in, were already at the plane. These limos were taking Axl, Doug, and a few others back from the U2 concert.

Oops.

Axl smirked.

But Doug laid into me.

He pinched his thumb and his index finger together and said, "I have this much respect for people who drink and get drunk."

That night changed my life.

Literally.

Axl was very cool about it. In fact, he laughed about it on the plane and told me not to worry about it. But Doug was my buddy from Air Supply, and I was hired because I wasn't "that guy." And I let him down.

But it was a blessing. I slowed down my drinking a lot for the rest of the tour, and when we got off the road, after the tour was over, after one or two more binges with Natasha, I remembered what Doug said that night. And in 1994, my wife and I quit drinking.

We haven't had a drink since.

I did not have an "official" drinking problem, but I'm sure it could have easily headed that way. I mean, come on, I was on tour with Guns N' Roses. That could have gone so bad. But it didn't.

That night changed my thinking, and I am fully convinced that my wife and I are successful today because we don't drink. We wake up every day, sharp, ready to conquer the day. And we feel great.

We think about having a glass of wine again, someday, and maybe we will. But thanks to that night in Oklahoma City, I gained a new outlook on where I wanted to go in life, and who I wanted to be.

Thanks, Doug.

Doug Goldstein and me. Yes, we're really close friends.

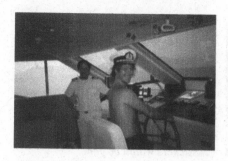

Me on a yacht in the Greek Islands. MTV paid for this excursion.

Duff and Matt doing an interview for MTV on the yacht off the Greek Islands.

Tour Manager John Reese about to throw me into the waters just off the Greek Islands. Tour accountant Jerry Gemdron looks on.

Sitting in the cockpit of our plane, the MGM Grand. You get all sorts of perks when touring with Guns N' Roses.

August Jakobsson, me, and Kirt Klingerman (management team) standing outside our MGM plane. Notice the bumper stickers. We shared the plane with Bruce Springsteen and U2, and every time the plane would come back from traveling with them, our bumper stickers would be gone.

Duff and Slash (hair) enjoying the spread of food on the MGM Grand.

This is what was always waiting for us when Guns N' Roses arrived at an airport. The limos would drive right onto the tarmac and take us either directly to the hotel or to the venue.

HOTELS

When I first started dating Natasha I had been on the road with Guns N' Roses for about a year. We had met on a blind date set up by my sister, Pamela, on August 14, 1991. I found out Natasha only went out on that date with me because my sister was her friend. It was definitely a sympathy date.

Women!

Anyway, we had a great time on the date, but I was still seeing Kim, and Natasha was being stalked by a guy living in a Dumpster outside her Beverly Hills apartment. I personally didn't want to get involved in that situation, so we parted ways until fate brought us back together exactly one year later to the date. And we owe all that to James Hetfield, lead singer of Metallica, which I will explain later in this book.

So I'm dating Natasha, and I am really in love. It's the beginning of our relationship and I'm head over heels. I wanted nothing to

do with strip clubs and other women. I knew that this was it—
that I would marry Natasha Kozmovsky. I was sure of it. In fact I
was so sure of it that after only six weeks I asked her to marry me
on October 6, 1992.

She said yes.

It was perfect timing because I was able to stay in Los Angeles
for a while because we were on a break. But our next leg of the
tour was in South America and we would be gone for a while.

I decided it would be a great idea to bring her out on the road
for a few weeks while we were touring South America. Since
we had our own plane the flights from city to city wouldn't cost
me anything, and there was room on the plane, so I figured this
would be a great opportunity to really bond and get to know
each other.

I had Natasha meet me in Caracas, Venezuela. I still remember her getting off the plane and me thinking to myself, *I'm the
luckiest guy in the world.* I still think so. Natasha is beautiful both
inside and out.

We walked hand in hand to the baggage claim, but I got the
feeling that something was wrong. She was happy to see me, but
I just felt something wasn't right. Even though the entire time we
were just waiting for her bags I felt the hundreds of people around
us, staring at us, thinking to themselves get a room, please.

Her bags never arrived. I kept thinking this wasn't a good start
to this trip.

Little did I know it was about to get much worse.

We took the limo and headed back to the hotel, sans luggage. I
figured the limo would be a nice touch, trying to impress a woman
whom I found out later couldn't care less about materialistic crap.
But I was with Guns N' Roses, so I was set to impress my fiancée.

Still, something seemed "off."

And then it happened.

About five minutes into the ride Natasha pulled out a *Life* magazine article and showed it to me.

"Did you read this?"

Immediately it all made sense—why she was acting so cold.

About a month prior, a writer from *Life* came out and toured with Guns N' Roses for a week to see and write about what really goes on during a world tour with a hugely successful rock n' roll band. The article shared what "they thought" really went on behind the scenes in a very long and very detailed article along with a few "interesting" pictures. The article was pretty revealing: backstage parties, sex, drugs (not really), and rock n' roll. You know, the typical article about "bad boys" on the road. But here's the deal—we were all on our best behavior that week, at least most of us were, so it was not really an accurate account. Thank goodness the writer never saw what really happened on the road.

But unfortunately, Natasha did.

Prior to that article, I had told Natasha that although touring with Guns N' Roses was an incredible experience, and that there were some wild things that happened, it still was a business first, and the band and the management took their responsibilities very seriously. And for the most part that was true. But there were some nights that were wilder than a fraternity party on the most raging campuses across America. But I didn't want to lose Natasha, and I personally was done with all that "other stuff" because I was truly in love.

"Oh you read that, huh?" I said.

"Oh yeah, I read it."

And Elaine, her best friend, had read it, too. Elaine had tried to persuade Natasha not to come to meet me, and to seriously reconsider marrying me, because who would want to be married to a guy who toured with Guns N' Roses?

Ouch.

Elaine is also married to Ray Parker Jr., of "Ghostbusters" fame. Ray and Elaine are great friends of ours to this day. But I had to dispel Elaine's and *Life* magazine's theory of touring in one limousine ride, otherwise this was going to be a very uncomfortable three weeks.

And to make matters worse, Elaine had "experience" in the field of backstage parties because Ray Parker Jr. toured for a living.

This was not going to be easy.

"Honey, you know not to believe everything you read. The story was embellished."

"Well, we'll see. I have three weeks out here, so I will see for myself," she reminded me.

So there I was, praying that the next three weeks would be the calmest weeks Guns N' Roses ever spent on the road. No naked women, no raging parties, nothing but good old rock music.

Yeah, that was going to happen.

We arrived at the hotel and I introduced everyone to Natasha, and everyone got along beautifully. All the band members are truly respectful to wives, girlfriends, and family. The first time my mom met Slash was in New York City. Slash was in the hotel lobby, and I walked in with my mom. Without any prompting, Slash walked over to my mom with open arms, and said, "Mom." Then, he gave her a big hug.

She fell in love with Slash from that moment on.

And Natasha did as well—with everyone in the band and the crew. They were very welcoming. Especially Axl. Axl loved when Natasha would come out to visit to get a woman's perspective on life, probably because he was sick of my perspective all the time.

That night there was no show, so Natasha and I just hung in the room, ordered room service, and just chilled. She was feeling much better after having met the guys.

Only wish that would have lasted at least one night.

When you tour with a band like Guns N' Roses, you must be on your toes 24/7. We had tons of security everywhere we went, and no one could come onto our hotel floor. We would book every room on a hotel floor, and most floors needed a special key to get to.

Another tool for our high security was our walkie-talkies. We all had to bring our walkie-talkies wherever we went, and they had to be on at all times—no exceptions. If you were with a woman, in the middle of "it," and someone needed you and called on the walkie-talkie, you were expected to stop what you were doing and address the situation immediately.

I always left my walkie-talkie right next to my bed because I was mostly responsible for Axl Rose. If something happened to him, there would be cancelled shows, disappointed fans, and a lot of people out of work. So out of everyone, I needed my walkie-talkie on at all times, and I had to be available 24/7 no matter what.

That included when Natasha was on the road as well.

On this special night, when Natasha and I got to hold each other because we missed each other, that walkie-talkie started making a sound.

I didn't really think anything of it—even though it was about two in the morning. I thought to myself it was probably Duff wanting someone to get him a drink because he ran out of vodka.

No luck.

Coming from the walkie-talkie were these now-famous words.

"Gentlemen, the ladies are here. Let the games begin."

I had no idea who it was, but at that point it really didn't matter.

And with that I jumped out of bed and started fumbling with my walkie-talkie, trying my best to turn it off.

Natasha stared at me and sternly said, "Leave it on."

I did.

Then from the walkie-talkie we heard giggling. A lot of giggling, by a lot of girls.

I was screwed. I knew where this was going, and there was no way to explain it.

But it was even worse than I thought. All of a sudden, outside my hotel room door I heard what sounded like a stampede. And more giggling.

I turned to Natasha, who had the most interesting smile on her face. I didn't know if she thought this was funny, or if she was about to kill me even though I had nothing to do with this.

"I'm going to go see what's going on," I said out loud, much to my surprise.

"You're not going anywhere, Craig."

Before that moment my name was always "Honey" or "Peach." Now it was "Craig." Just like when my mom was pissed at me as a kid.

But I did have to do my job and make sure everything was okay. So I opened my hotel door, and I saw about fifty naked women right outside my door, walking down the hall. To where, I don't know. I could only guess at this point.

I wanted to leave my door open for at least a few seconds, but thought better of it.

I turned to Natasha and she was still smiling.

"Honey, this has never happened before." And while I was telling the truth, *I* didn't even believe me.

"Do you want to go with them?"

Boy was that a loaded question.

Obviously I stayed with Natasha, and while it took her a little time to get used to the road, she was totally okay. Truth be told, that was the only night something like that happened. I found out the next day, because I just had to know, that the promoter in South America thought it would be really cool and impressive to empty a whorehouse out and bring them all to the hotel via bus . . . naked.

Yes, right through the hotel lobby, into the elevators, and onto our floor.

You don't see that every day. Not even with Guns N' Roses.

Me and Natasha in Cancun, Mexico. During the tour I actually had the chance to enjoy a few days off with my wife-to-be Natasha. Oh, I wish I still had that much hair!

PAPARAZZI—GERMANY

We were in Germany and Natasha was out on the road with us again for a few dates. I loved it when Natasha came out on the road because Axl would pretty much let me be with her, and Robert would take the lead for a while. It was almost like we were on vacation, even though I still had to go to the shows, and I was still responsible for doing my job.

Most of the time we tended to stay in the hotel, because going out on the town with Axl took a lot of hard work. We had to pre-screen where we were going, we had to make sure we had security, and I had to coordinate transportation. It wasn't like Axl and I could just take a walk during the middle of the day, in a city he was about to play a show in front of 80,000 raging fans.

But I could take a walk with Natasha.

And so we did.

We went right out the front of the hotel, hand in hand, and just went for a walk. That's it, a simple walk. But for me, it was so refreshing. It's amazing when you can appreciate the simple things in life, and while fame has some great perks, many celebrities can't take a walk in a city in the middle of the day. Axl would have been mauled in seconds.

We went window shopping, walking down a busy city street, and we got the feeling that someone was following us. I had really long hair at the time (see picture on the previous page) and many of us on the road did as well, and we were sometimes mistaken for members of the band. Plus, I was wearing really cool, ripped jeans. At the very least people knew we were probably part of the staff or crew. We kept walking and every once in a while I turned around, but no one was there, at least no one who looked suspicious. We kept hearing a camera shutter sound, but no one was ever there.

We knew what was happening. A German photographer had probably mistaken me for a member of the band, but Natasha and I didn't let it bother us. We kept walking and milked it. In fact, we milked it so much that people on the streets could see the photographer following us, so they stared as well, trying to figure out who we were.

We went to a lake and fed some geese, you know all those things rock stars do on a regular basis.

After a few hours we headed back to the hotel. And our photographer friend was still there, following us.

That night Guns N' Roses performed.

The next day, Natasha and I got something to eat in the lobby. A man came up to us, seeming a little pissed, and handed me a large manila envelope.

When you're on tour with Guns N' Roses, in a foreign country, and there is security everywhere, the last thing you want is to be handed a large manila envelope by someone who seems a bit off.

But it didn't feel like there were any drugs in the envelope.

The guy said, "Here you go."

I reluctantly took the package.

Awkward silence.

I finally said, "What is it?"

"Apparently you're not famous. So here you go."

And he left. He still seemed a little perturbed as he walked away.

I looked at Natasha and said, "Okay, that was weird."

I opened the envelope, and inside were about 500 pictures of Natasha and me on our little jaunt through the city the day before.

Classic.

Just like I figured—he thought I was in the band and he wanted to capture my day on the town. Unfortunately for him, it was a total waste of four hours.

I imagined the meeting he probably had with his boss after showing him the pictures. The boss probably said, "Who the hell is this guy?" And he probably said, "A guy from Guns N' Roses, right?"

And he was probably immediately removed from the office and became the laughingstock of German paparazzi that day.

But I personally appreciated him very much. He documented my entire walk with my fiancée through the city and the park at no charge. For that, I say thank you, Mr. Paparazzi Man, whoever you were, for the awesome pictures.

TOWER RECORDS

Ah, the power of touring with a band like Gun N' Roses. If you used the power right, and were respectful, you could get whatever you wanted, whenever you wanted.

Case in point—Hollywood, 1993.

I was staying at Hotel Nikko in Los Angeles with Natasha. We were off for a few weeks, and when we were off, the band put us up at a hotel in Los Angeles. It's funny, Slash has a house in Los Angeles. But he used to stay with us at the hotel. He had been on the road for so long that he enjoyed staying at a hotel even though his house was just a few miles away. Probably because he would miss me too much if he didn't see me for a few weeks.

Out of all the guys in the band, Slash was the one I used to party with the most. Not that it was a lot, but when I went out I would usually go out with Slash and his gang. If I went out with Axl, I would have to work, but with Slash, all I had to do was drink and party. I could do that very well.

So, I was staying at Hotel Nikko, and Natasha and I were listening to music on my portable stereo. We were listening to Queen, because we both love Queen. We were talking about obscure Queen songs and I asked her if she ever heard the song "You Take My Breath Away." She hadn't.

I wanted to play that song for her right then and there, but I didn't have that specific album. It was the perfect moment to play that song and I couldn't play it. Back then there was no iTunes.

I was used to getting everything I wanted, the second I wanted it. Not because of me, but simply because I was with Guns N' Roses, and more specifically, I was with Axl Rose. If Axl wanted something, I could get it within minutes. For example, one time, Axl wanted me to find him an English-speaking ear, nose, and throat doctor in Czechoslovakia.

Axl had a very sore throat, if I remember correctly. He really wasn't feeling well, and he was tempted to cancel the show. But it was like an hour or two before the show, and many of the 80,000 people were already in their seats.

Axl turned to me and said, "Get me an English-speaking ENT in thirty minutes or I'm not doing the show tonight."

Imagine the pressure. And this was without the Internet and a cell phone.

But I was on it. I called people to call people. I called hospitals, I called the local police (who I had met the night before in my limo accident), I called drug stores, anything I could think of. We had a translator touring with us, and I had him with me for the next ten minutes, helping me out on the phones. And if I remember correctly, someone backstage had a friend of a friend, and we had him call his friend the "English-speaking ENT." He was about fifteen minutes away. I offered him a few thousand dollars if he would drop everything and come right away. He arrived backstage within fifteen minutes and helped Axl get better almost immediately.

They say that pressure turns coal into diamonds, and there was a lot of pressure that night, but it was one hell of a show.

So, I was trained, and I realized that I could get anything I wanted because of the status of Guns N' Roses in the early 90s.

My Natasha wanted to listen to "You Take My Breath Away." Well, actually it was more me wanting her to hear the song, but who's keeping track?

Problem was it was 11:50 p.m., and I knew that Tower Records closed at midnight. I had no car, and no limo waiting for me out front, and a taxi would take way too long.

So I called Tower Records.

An employee answered the phone. "Towers Records, may I help you?"

"Yes, okay, this will seem like a weird call at first, but I promise you that what I'm about to tell you is true, so please don't hang up."

The guy said, "I work at Tower Records. Nothing you say will surprise me."

Touché.

I told him that I worked with Guns N' Roses, which was true.

I told him that I was currently on tour with Guns N' Roses, which was true.

I told him that I specifically worked with Axl Rose. Also very true.

And then I told him that Axl wanted to hear a song by Queen, and that we didn't have the album. Okay, that part wasn't true. But I lied for love.

I went on to say that I couldn't leave the hotel because I couldn't leave Axl there alone because we had no other security. But we needed that Queen album. And that Axl really wanted it tonight.

He was silent. I wasn't sure if he was silent because he didn't believe me, or that he was talking to someone who worked with Axl Rose.

"Hello?"

"Yes, I'm still here."

"So, I was wondering if it would be possible for me to give you a credit card over the phone, and then pay you to drive the CD over to my hotel."

Silence again.

But then all of a sudden he said, "I can do that."

I immediately did the happy dance.

Natasha shook her head in disbelief.

Then the guy said, "But we don't take credit cards over the phone."

Damn.

"Okay, how about this . . . How about you pay for the CD with your money, then drive it over here. I'll pay you back for the CD, and I'll give you an extra $100 for your trouble."

Think about it. I had just asked, probably a teenager, to spend his hard-earned money on a CD, and then drive it to my hotel, to a stranger, in hopes that I would be there, and in hopes of getting $100 as well. It was a different world in 1993. I would not suggest doing this today.

But he agreed. And about thirty minutes later he came to my hotel door, and handed me the Queen CD. I handed him $120 and an autographed picture of Guns N' Roses.

He was happy, and I was happy, and very thankful.

I played the song for Natasha, and you can probably guess what happened next in our dimly lit hotel room.

WAITER WANTS AXL'S AUTOGRAPH

Just like in airports, the hotel staff got very excited when Guns N' Roses arrived. John Reese, our tour manager, or Bill Greer, the head of the GNR security team, would always wait for the band's arrival at a hotel. When we arrived, John or Bill handed me my key and Axl's key, and we would head straight into the elevator and right into our rooms.

If we waited or stalled for even one second in the lobby a crowd would form around Axl (and the rest of the band for that matter) in seconds.

I would open Axl's door, and while he got settled I made sure everything in the room was in order—checking to see if his favorite food and drinks were stocked in the refrigerator, and checking to see if there were any crazy fans hiding in closets, showers, or under the bed.

When everything checked out I went next door and opened my door, and got ready for the upcoming show. Our luggage would arrive within the hour, delivered straight to our doors. Within the next few hours Axl would come into my room and we would order room service.

Sometimes he'd hang and wait for it in my room, and we'd just talk and/or watch television. Other times he'd head back into his room and I'd call him when the food arrived. We usually ate together, along with Robert, Earl, and sometimes, Steve.

On this particular day, somewhere in Europe (sorry I forget—it might have been Italy), Axl ordered and went back to his room. He wasn't in a good mood because his throat was bothering him and he had a show that night.

About forty-five minutes later our food arrived, rolled into my room by a very nice room service waiter dressed in a sharp black tuxedo. We usually stayed in five-star hotels, and the hotel staff was always dressed to the nines.

The waiter told me that he was a huge fan of Guns N' Roses. By my estimate he looked about fifty-five years old, so I found it weird that he was a huge fan, but who was I to judge? He asked me if the food was for Axl Rose. I said it was. He got all giddy.

Picture a fifty-five-year-old man getting giddy. It ain't pretty.

"Can I get Axl's autograph?" asked the waiter.

I said to him, "Today really isn't a good day."

His giddiness left his body.

To save the waiter from bursting out in tears, I added, "But let me ask him after the show tonight for you. What's your name?"

I wrote his name on my pad of paper.

I personally don't understand the importance of getting an autograph from a celebrity. I've met thousands of famous people in my life and have asked for an autograph only once. And I didn't even ask her in person.

In my late teens I went to see Olivia Newton-John in concert with my childhood buddy Steve Dantzig. We were in about the tenth row, center stage. I loved Olivia Newton-John.

So the day of the concert I did the dweebiest thing I have ever done—I wrote her a letter and bought her a single rose. My plan was to walk up to her, while she was onstage. She would read my letter while singing one of her songs, and she would stop the concert, lean over, give me a peck on the cheek and autograph my Olivia Newton-John program.

We all know that never happened, so I just tossed my letter and rose onstage near her feet. I am positive now, from touring with bands for over ten years, that that letter never made it to her dressing room.

After the show I thought to myself, *What was I doing?* It had felt so weird that I decided to never ask for another autograph again.

I have nothing against people that do it, but it's just not me. I guess that's why I fit in with Air Supply and Guns N' Roses so well. I just treated them like regular people.

THAT IS WHAT ROCK STARS WANT. To be treated like regular people.

Asking for an autograph is just awkward. It's pretty much a no-win situation for the person asking for the autograph because the celebrity often thinks, *Oh, I gotta sign more stuff.* Many of them hate it. They love that they have fans, but many celebrities hate signing autographs after a while.

The room service waiter had an idea. "Maybe I can knock on his door and ask him right now?"

I wasn't sure if the waiter either ignored what I just said, or if he didn't speak English very well.

"Did you just hear what I said? Again, today really isn't a good day. He's tired and just wants to be left alone."

"I understand," he said.

"Good, we're on the same page. I promise, if you don't ask him now, I will get you an autograph tonight after the show."

I figured that the worst-case scenario would be that Axl wouldn't want to sign anything after the show, but that I could sign one of Axl's 8 x 10s myself if I had to. I had done it many times before.

"Okay, you promise?" pleaded the waiter.

"I promise."

And with that Axl walked into my room.

As if I didn't exist, the waiter walked right into Axl's face, took out the room service bill, turned it over, and asked Axl for his autograph.

"Dude, are you serious?" I yelled.

The waiter ignored me.

"Axl, I just told him that I would get him an autograph later tonight."

So Axl grabbed a handful of fries, and I took the waiter by the arm and tried to escort him out of the room.

But this guy wasn't going down without a fight.

He squirmed out of my grip and went right back in Axl's face.

He was so rude about it that I was shocked that Axl didn't pop him in the face right there. But Axl just remained calm and ate his French fries.

I grabbed the waiter around the waist and hoisted him up in the air. He screamed, "Axl, just one autograph, please, I love you!" as I tossed him out of my room, and slammed the door.

Axl and I then sat down to eat as if nothing just happened.

Except I think Axl said something like, "That was weird."

And then we watched television.

About ten minutes later, there was a knock at my door. Axl and I were still eating dinner.

I yelled, "Who is it?"

No answer.

I thought to myself that there was no way the guy would come back.

I looked through the peephole, and it was him.

"Are you serious?" I said through the door.

No answer.

"Dude, I can see you through the peephole, I know it's you."

"Please, sir, can I have Axl's autograph?"

Axl and I just started cracking up.

"I gotta say, the guy is persistent," I added.

The best thing about touring with a band like Guns N' Roses is that nearly all situations can be handled in less than ten seconds.

I got on my walkie-talkie, and I called for security to remove the guy standing at my door.

Within four seconds Axl and I heard the waiter screaming, "Let me go. What are you doing? Put me down. Owwww!"

Axl and I continued to enjoy our dinner.

I did not give him an autographed picture after the show.

THE $5,000 PHONE CALL

Cell phones were just hitting the market in the early 90s. Unfortunately, many of us did not have one while on tour, including me. So, believe it or not, we actually used hotel room phones to make phone calls. These days phones are more like decorations in hotels rooms, but back then, although very expensive, that was how you made calls. When we were overseas, calling from a hotel room was way too expensive. So we had to be creative when calling our girlfriends in the States.

Most of the time, during or after a show, I went into the production trailer and used the phones in there. The promoters usually paid for those expenses. But sometimes I wanted to talk to my sweetie from my hotel room. One night in Germany, I got screwed with my hotel room. It wasn't ready yet, even though it was way past check-in time.

The hotel gave me a temporary room for three hours, and they said that I could use the phone in that room for free because of my inconvenience. I took full advantage of the situation and spoke to Natasha for three hours straight.

When we checked out two days later I received my hotel bill, and much to my surprise there was a charge on it for about $5,000. Yes, $5,000 for one phone call. The fees had fees, and the up charges had up charges.

Luckily, again, I was great at negotiating, because after a few hours of begging and pleading (and maybe even shedding a tear), I got them down to $50, plus some autographed pictures.

CHILI & CHEESE

Ninety-nine percent of the time we ordered room service for breakfast and lunch. Dinner would either be at the show, or at a place like Denny's after the show at about three in the morning. Unfortunately, room service was very expensive because we usually stayed in nice hotels, but we received $50-a-day per diem to cover costs like that. I wish I would have saved that money, but it was hard for me to get out of the hotel to hit the local McDonald's to save a few bucks.

Buenos Aires, Argentina.

About 80,000 people were at the concert about fifteen minutes from the hotel. Earl, Robert, Steve, and I were still at the hotel waiting for Axl to get ready, and everyone else was at the gig.

Axl was a little hungry, so he came into my room and asked me to order him a quick dinner. That stressed me out a little because we should've been leaving right about then, but now we had to wait for room service.

Axl and I often talked about life, about world issues, about our girlfriends. But we rarely talked about the upcoming show, or what time we would have to leave to get there on time. I always had to "squeeze" that into the conversation . . . "Yeah, I agree, Axl. That sucks. Oh, by the way, we have to leave at eight o'clock tonight because there's an early curfew."

He would just go on with the conversation as if I hadn't spoken. But I knew he heard me. We performed this little routine for more than two years. And most of the time he would leave within an hour of the time we needed to leave, and because of the "buffer" we were good.

But on this night we were pushing the envelope a little.

"Can you order me some chili and cheese?"

I said, "Sure."

I grabbed the menu and looked for something that resembled chili and cheese.

Nothing.

I don't even think a hotel in America would serve chili and cheese, so I thought that this ain't gonna be easy in South America.

I called room service, and I ordered chili and cheese. Of course, their main language is Spanish, but they do speak English as well. But just to be safe, because it wasn't on the menu, I described exactly what chili and cheese was.

"Chili and cheese."

"Yes, Mr. Duswalt."

"And we need it fast, because we have to get to a show. It's for Axl Rose."

"Yes, Mr. Duswalt."

"Do you understand chili and cheese?"

"Yes, Mr. Duswalt."

"Are you sure? It sounds like you might be confused."

"Yes, Mr. Duswalt."

As I hung up I knew this wasn't going to go well. I had that feeling.

I turned to Earl. "He was just 'yessing' me. We're screwed."

Earl just smiled. His job was to protect Axl, and he knew he wouldn't get any crap if we were late. It was all on my ass.

Thirty minutes later, nothing.

Forty-five minutes, nothing.

Doug called me on the walkie-talkie, which although he was fifteen minutes away, was coming in clear as a bell.

"Deuce."

My nickname was "Deuce" because I used to be a very good tennis player. I got the name while touring with Air Supply because I always kicked everyone's ass in tennis. Doug and I toured together with Air Supply, so he still called me that.

"Go, Doug."

"How close are you?"

Earl just smiled.

"Uh, we're still waiting for room service."

Silence. We were supposed to be there about an hour ago.

"Should be here any minute," I continued.

"What did he order?"

"Chili and cheese. He just wanted a quick bite."

"Have him eat it in the limo."

"Got it."

I looked at Earl, "You want to tell him to eat it in the limo?" Earl just smiled.

"That's what I figured." I picked up the hotel phone and dialed room service.

"I ordered chili and cheese almost an hour ago, and I needed it fast. Is it coming?"

"Yes, Mr. Duswalt."

"Okay, say 'Yes, Mr. Duswalt' one more time. I dare you."

"Yes, Mr. Duswalt."

Well that didn't work.

I hung up and told Earl I was going to the hotel kitchen.

And with that, there was a knock on my door.

"Finally."

I opened the door and there he was, my knight in shining armor. I had never been more happy to see a room service waiter.

I motioned for him to come in and to put the tray on the edge of the bed. He did. And as all room service waiters do, he lifted the metal lid off the dinner plate to reveal the chef's creation. And there it was, in all its glory.

Chili and cheese.

I just stared at it. Earl just stared at it. We both turned to the waiter who had a big smile on his face.

He proudly exclaimed, "Chili and cheese."

And there on the plate was exactly what I ordered, chili and cheese. Yes, a block of cheddar cheese surrounded by six whole red-hot chili peppers.

I immediately felt like screaming at the waiter, but he was just the messenger, and it wasn't his fault. I tried to explain to him that this wasn't chili and cheese, and he disagreed.

He pointed to the whole chilies and said, "Chili."

Then he pointed to the block of cheddar cheese and said, "Cheese."

"Chili and cheese."

How do you argue with that?

So I went into what would become my patented RockStar training survival mode.

I thanked the waiter, signed the bill, and escorted him out of the room because I didn't want him to see what was going to take place next. Plus, I didn't want him to be in harm's way.

I had a plan, but it wasn't going to be pretty.

When Axl hit the stage he was extremely high-octane energy for more than two hours. Axl gave it his all, 100 percent, all the time. But to do that, to give people a great show, he liked to get "worked up" before going onstage.

I knew that showing him the plate of chilies and a block of cheese might set him off, but I didn't want him to go into a show with negative energy.

"Deuce," called Doug on the walkie-talkie.

"Not now, Doug."

I turned my walkie-talkie off, and I put my plan into action.

I took the plate of chilies and cheese, and a few other plates and water glasses, and walked into the hallway.

I threw the plate of chili and cheese, and the extra plates, and the water glasses against the wall, smashing them into a thousand pieces. It made a huge noise.

Axl came running out of his room.

"What the hell was that?"

I pointed to the chili and cheese strewn all over the floor.

"They screwed up. I ordered chili and cheese and this is what they brought up. So, I got pissed at the waiter and I threw the plates at him in disgust. Sorry, I lost my temper."

Axl said something like, "Dude, you gotta calm down."

"I know," I agreed.

Then Axl said, "Let's get out of here."

And we left for the venue.

And that, my friends, is how you handle a bad situation in a foreign country. RockStar-style.

WHAT WOULD YOU DO FOR $1,000?

Believe it or not, it's easy to get bored on the road, even on one of the biggest tours in the history of rock. Very bored. The thirty of us in the band and the entourage saw each other 365 days a year, twenty-four hours a day, seven days a week. There's only so much you can talk about, especially when you're cooped up in your room because thousands of fans are lining the streets outside the hotel. It was so bad that strip clubs even became boring.

Craig, Duff, and Gilby after wrestling match.

So, what to do?

Once in a while we would have wrestling matches. On page 67 is the end of a wrestling match between me, Duff, and Gilby. There usually wasn't a winner, but it was always a great way to burn off the recently ingested alcohol in our systems.

Another hobby we all loved took place backstage either before or after the show. Let me first say that this was by far the stupidest thing I ever participated in because of the size of the guys I would play against.

Picture this: Me, a six foot, 190-pound guy in pretty decent shape, having a punching contest with one of the members of our security team, which had an average height of six-foot-two, and an average weight of about 260 pounds.

I'm talking big guys.

What we would do is stand opposite each other with the outsteps of our right feet touching each other's. Once positioned we could not move. We would each then lean back and try to avoid getting hit, while at the same time trying to hit our opponent's upper right arm with our right fists as hard as we could.

And I mean, as hard as we could.

Grown men, responsible for a multimillion-dollar world tour, acting like little kids on a playground.

And me, the stupidest one of all, playing this game against these huge guys.

I usually got a few shots in, but all they had to do was connect once and it was over. I had multiple bruises on my arms for about six months of the tour until, thankfully, I played my last match.

It was against Duff's security guy. His name was Rick Beaman, and his nickname was Truck, and that right there should be enough description for you to imagine his size. Great guy—pretty much a big teddy bear.

Truck and I lined up and went about thirty seconds' worth of missed punches and slight connections, but no pain yet. The one thing I had going for me was speed. These guys were huge, but I was fast.

All of a sudden I decided to go for it and I nailed Truck with a good shot to his arm. Unfortunately, it was as if a fly had landed on his arm. No ill effect from the punch at all. But because I lunged at him and connected, it left me wide open, and he took his shot. The shot only grazed my right arm, and for one millisecond I was grateful that he kinda missed . . . until the continuing progress of that punch hit me in my face, more specifically, my jaw.

Down I went.

I saw stars, and for a few seconds I didn't know what hit me, but it felt like a truck. (Sorry, couldn't resist.)

And that was it. After that night I retired from the stupidest game ever invented by a bunch of bored men on tour with a famous band.

Because I retired from that game, I was hoping someone would come up with more creative ways to have fun on the road to keep me entertained.

Enter Axl Rose.

One night in Buenos Aires, Axl thought it would be a good idea to offer one of the members of the entourage a few hundred dollars cash to run naked in the streets outside the front of our hotel, in front of hundreds of screaming fans. Most people would think this would be enough to earn a few hundred dollars.

Not Axl.

After the naked man ran in the street, Axl wanted him to shake the hand of an Argentinean police officer.

I thought that whoever did this would experience, firsthand, *Midnight Express*. I personally wouldn't do this in the United States, but to do it in a foreign county? Not a chance.

Gene Kirkland didn't think it would be a problem.

Gene was one of the two photographers for Guns N' Roses. He and Robert John basically documented the entire tour in pictures, taking thousands of shots during the three-year journey.

I'm not sure how much money Gene got paid on the road, but obviously he felt that it wouldn't hurt to pick up some extra cash.

But Gene was in negotiation mode. He wanted $1,000.

Axl agreed, and the dare was on.

Gene agreed that for $1,000 he would walk outside the front of the hotel in a bath towel, toss aside the towel to reveal his nakedness, run over to a police officer, and shake his hand.

Simple.

Within seconds we all got on our walkie-talkies, and told everyone to come to the lobby immediately to watch Gene go to jail, because in my mind, if his did this, that's exactly where he was going.

The photos on page 73 show the sequence of the event.

Gene left the lobby, headed up to his room to get ready, and within minutes the band members and the entire entourage were in the lobby ready to witness Gene's last hour of freedom.

The documentary crew came running down to the lobby; they had basically documented the entire tour to date, and they weren't about to miss this fine piece of Guns N' Roses lore.

The hundreds of fans lined up behind a metal fence barrier were also ready, anticipating that something "cool" was about to happen, even though they didn't know what.

The elevator bell dinged, and Gene stepped out in the lobby wearing only a white bath towel and a tie. The tie was a great touch—class personified.

Axl flashed ten crisp, new $100 bills, and we were off to take our positions outside the front of the hotel.

I could tell that Gene was freaking out by the horrified look on his face, because I think reality had just set in, but it was too late to turn back. There were too many people watching.

Axl pointed to a police officer standing across the street and instructed Gene that that was the officer he was to shake hands with. Of course Axl chose the meanest looking one.

By then every one of us was advising Gene how to do this. As if it were rocket science. We told him a bunch of unnecessary crap: how to throw the towel off, to watch out for the curb, and to make sure the handshake was firm. We all just wanted to be part of it. This was fun for us, and especially fun for the band. Playing in front of 80,000 people? That happens every day. But having a guy in the entourage run naked through the streets of Buenos Aires? Now, that's a great time.

Without notice, as if he had been shot out of a cannon, Gene was off. He pulled off his towel and ran naked across the hotel parking lot on a beeline to the pre-chosen police officer. He approached the officer, smiling the entire time, reached his hand out, and waited for a handshake.

The police officer didn't really know what was happening for a second, but amazingly he reached out and shook hands with Gene.

I was in shock. The police officer actually shook hands with him. The officer started to smile, and for a split-second I thought Gene would be okay, that they wouldn't throw his naked ass in jail.

Gene turned to us and smiled.

But that was only a fleeting moment, because about two seconds later, two police officers grabbed Gene, each taking hold of his upper arms, and proceeded to guide him up against the outside of the hotel wall. Gene dropped his towel, and the police officers made him spread his legs and put his two hands up on the wall.

We all laughed, because it was hysterical, but we all thought the same thing. Gene was going to jail. We didn't know exactly how long a sentence is for running naked through the streets in Buenos Aires, but we all knew he wasn't going to be free in the near future.

He was screwed.

Then something weird happened. Obviously protocol at this point is to frisk the perpetrator, and they did. But he was naked.

What were they frisking?

And as they were "frisking" Gene, the police officers couldn't hold it in any longer, and they started laughing.

Axl and Doug cracked up as well. The tension was broken.

But most of us still thought that this wasn't going to end well, until Doug told us what was up.

Doug had paid off the police officers to fake arrest Gene and after a few moments set him free.

Only in Argentina.

The police officers were in on the ruse, and so were Axl and Doug, and maybe even a few others. I had thought for sure that Gene was going to jail. More amazing was that Gene had no idea that this was planned out. He thought, in a moment of insanity, that he would be allowed to walk over to a police officer in a foreign country, naked, and not get in trouble. When he was tossed up against the wall, reality set in and he said he thought to himself, *I'm screwed.*

But luckily it was all a setup.

Gene put his towel back on, adjusted his tie, grabbed the $1,000 from Axl, and headed back to the lobby bar. A richer man with a lesson learned.

Axl getting ready to award $1,000 to our tour photographer, Gene Kirkland, if he runs up to a cop (naked), and offers to shake his hand . . . in Buenos Aires, Argentina.

Gene getting frisked after he shakes the police officers' hands. What are they frisking?

Gene, the victor, and $1,000 richer.

MY TOWEL

Speaking of nudity . . .

Nudity was a huge part of the Guns N' Roses tour. Every night there was a naked person backstage. Most of the time it was a woman, unless Shannon Hoon of Blind Melon or Adam Clayton of U2 were around.

Because we were really bored, whenever someone had a chance to get someone naked in public, they jumped on it.

And because we had our own floor 95 percent of the time, it was not uncommon for us to walk from room to room in our bathrobes or towels to say hi or to get something we needed. We all did it, and never thought anything of it.

So one day I walked down the hallway in my towel. I left my room door open because there was no place to carry my key. Like every other day I passed a few guys in the hallway and said a quick "hi."

Then I saw Ronnie, Slash's bodyguard, and Truck. But this time, unlike the other times, they wore an evil grin.

Faster than a hummingbird's wings, they swooped in on me, grabbed my towel, slammed my door shut, and ran into their respective rooms.

There I was, standing in the middle of the hallway of a five-star hotel, in all my glory, and there was nothing I could do about it.

I had to assume that Ronnie and Truck had gotten on their walkie-talkies, informed everyone the situation, and instructed them not to open their doors for me. I even saw someone open their doorway down the hall and pull their used room service tray *back* into their room so I wouldn't be able to use the metal dinner plate covers to cover my "parts."

I stood there in the hallway thinking that this was a no-win situation for me. To make matters worse, there was no show that evening, so no one really had to come out of their rooms for hours.

So I just paced the hallway, trying to come up with some sort of plan, trying to figure out how to get to the lobby to get another key to my room.

I walked over to the elevator area to use the house phone, but it was missing.

"Damn, they thought of everything," I whispered to myself.

There were some roses on a table that I thought I could strategically place but I ruled that out when I stuck myself with a thorn.

I thought about just walking over to knock on Earl's door but I knew he was probably in on it so he wouldn't let me in. I also thought that Earl wouldn't appreciate a naked man knocking on his door no matter what the situation.

This was a very embarrassing moment, with no solution in sight.

It really sucked, but it was about to get a little worse.

I heard the elevator doorbell go off, meaning someone was coming onto our floor. I prayed that it was a sympathetic person from our entourage.

It was. It was Sabrina, Axl's beautiful masseuse. I wasn't really embarrassed that Sabrina saw me naked because I had known her for so long. But it was definitely awkward.

Instead of being sympathetic, she just laughed. I kept hoping that she was laughing because I was naked, and not for any other reason.

"I need a towel," I said, stating the obvious.

And with that, someone stuck their head outside the door and said something; Sabrina acted immediately and ran into her room and closed her door.

Once again there was no solution in sight.

After about an hour of pacing, and patience running very thin, with nowhere else to turn, I finally came up with a great idea.

I pressed the button for an elevator, and I prayed really hard for this elevator to be empty.

The bell rang, and I took a chance, standing there naked as the door opened. It was indeed empty. Finally, something had gone in my favor.

I managed the courage to walk into the empty hotel elevator and I immediately hit the red STOP emergency button. I only had seconds until the dreaded alarm would go off. I feared that the elevator across the way would open and fifty people would stare at my naked ass.

So, in the elevator I looked down at the carpeting. I summoned all my superhuman strength, grabbed a little piece of the corner of the carpeting, and in one gigantic, superhuman pull, I ripped the entire piece up.

I felt like I had just won the lottery.

I have tried to do what I did that day in other hotel elevators across the country and I can never do it. That's how much adrenaline was running through my naked body.

Anyway, I wrapped the carpet around me, and did what any normal person would do. I took the elevator downstairs to the lobby, wrapped in carpeting. I looked like a toilet paper holder. I got off the elevator, and among the crowded lobby I shuffled over to the front desk, and casually asked the front desk clerk for another key to my room.

"You don't have ID with you, sir, do you?" asked the hotel employee.

I just smiled.

"Guns N' Roses?" he added.

"Yes."

And he handed me a key to my room. No questions asked. I guess he thought it was normal for a person touring with

Guns N' Roses to walk through the hotel lobby wearing only carpeting.

I went back to the elevators, and for some reason, no one waiting for the elevators wanted to get in with me.

So I pressed my floor button, I smiled, and the elevator doors closed.

I got up to my floor, shuffled to my room, dropped the carpeting, opened the door, and locked myself in my room for the next twenty-four hours.

By far, the most embarrassing day of my life.

DRUG SEARCHES & CLOSE CALLS

South America is a beautiful place. But for eighteen days in late 1992 so many weird things happened there that I was really glad when we came back to the United States for Christmas.

When we arrived in Caracas, the first thing that happened was Natasha lost her luggage. Oh, how we wished that was the worst of it. But not even close.

It poured the day before the show. In fact there was so much rain that the stage collapsed. They worked through the night to build a new stage and the concert was a huge success.

Two days after the Caracas show we were scheduled to leave for Bogotá. We made it, but because of a failed military coup by the Venezuela Air Force, half of the band's equipment didn't make the trip.

Glad we missed that event.

We were supposed to do two shows in Bogotá, but because the equipment didn't arrive in time for the first show, they decided to let two sold-out audiences into the second show. In hindsight, not a good idea.

Although it ended up being a very special show, it almost didn't happen.

Doug, the entourage, and the band were already at the venue in Bogotá, and reports came back that the stadium was packed beyond belief.

Earl, Robert, and I were waiting in my room for Axl to get ready. We were already about an hour late, but that was kind of normal.

Axl came into my room, still dressed in his shorts, and told me that he's not doing the show tonight.

And after dropping that bombshell, he headed back to his room.

The three of us look at one another.

"Anyone want to tell Doug?" I pleaded.

No takers. Apparently, this was my job so I had to handle it.

I got on my walkie-talkie, dreading what I was about to say.

"Doug."

"Go, Craig," Doug responded on his walkie-talkie from the venue about five miles away.

"Axl doesn't want to do the show."

Silence.

"Again?" Doug said.

I repeated, "Axl doesn't want to do the show."

Longer silence.

I turned to Earl. "I think he just had a heart attack."

Doug finally got back on the walkie-talkie. "Craig, call me from a landline."

I did.

On the hotel phone, "Hey, Doug."

Doug proceeded to tell me that there were about 80,000 people squeezed into a stadium that might fit 50,000. I might be exaggerating these numbers, and maybe Doug might have been as well, but you get the idea. If we cancelled at this last minute there would be a lot of pissed-off people.

Doug also reminded me that he'd just spoken with the police, and if Axl didn't arrive in the next fifteen minutes, they would make an announcement to the audience that the show was cancelled, and that they would not restrain the fans from destroying the stage.

My stress level reached new heights.

I'm a regular guy from a small town in Long Island and suddenly I was responsible for getting Axl Rose to a concert, otherwise equipment would be destroyed, and there was a good chance that people would die.

I had never told Axl that he *had* to do a show. But I knew I had to do it that night. It was not going to be a great conversation. I could tell when Axl walked into my room that he was not in a good mood. Something must have happened.

Doug then added a little detail that changed everything. "Oh, and let me remind you, Natasha is here backstage as well. And we're all not safe."

Well, that's all I needed to hear.

I grabbed the key to Axl's room, knocked on his door, and without waiting for an answer, opened his door with the key.

Axl was sitting on his couch in his dimly lit room.

"Axl, you have to do the show. If we're not there in fifteen minutes, they're going to release the audience, and Natasha is backstage, and so is your sister, Amy. Let's go."

And much to my surprise, he only said, "Fine." He headed to his bedroom to get dressed.

I walked out of his room, relieved.

I headed back into my room.

"Well that was easy," I bragged.

Robert asked, "What did you say?"

"I told him, 'Let's go,' and he said, 'Fine.'"

I left out the other details because it just sounded so awesome this way.

I got on the walkie-talkie.

"Doug."

"Go, Craig."

"We'll be there in fifteen minutes," I said proudly.

"Love you, buddy."

And with that Axl came into my room, and we left for the concert. Not a word was spoken in the car, and that was totally okay. I had one goal—get Axl to the show, and we were on our way.

The show was great. And something really cool happened this night.

"November Rain" had been the number-one song in Colombia for sixty straight weeks. That is almost unheard of in any market.

So, during the concert the band begins playing "November Rain," and it begins to rain.

The crowd went nuts. And although it's not really that safe to play electrical instruments in the rain with no cover, the band played on. I had chills. It was a very special moment, and knowing that Doug and I and maybe three others knew that this night almost didn't happen made it all the more special.

To top that? When the band finished playing "November Rain" it stopped raining.

Although the show was amazing, unfortunately a few injuries occurred. I don't know how they happened, all I know is that Steve, our traveling chiropractor, was called on to stitch up a Colombian Army guy's head, and also called on to stitch up Duff, who had apparently been hit by a bottle.

This is the ironic part. Steve couldn't find anything to use as an anesthetic to numb the injuries he had to stitch. But because he's on tour with Guns N' Roses, and even better, was in Colombia, he asked around if anyone had any cocaine so he could numb his patients.

He couldn't find any. Backstage at a Guns N' Roses concert, in Bogotá, Colombia, and there was no cocaine? Steve was in shock. How could this be?

But there was none to be found. So, he stitched them up without numbing. Now, don't get me wrong, I'm sure Duff never felt a thing. I'm pretty sure he was liquored up pretty good. But the poor Colombian Army guy . . .

Ouch.

As if all of this weren't enough, as we're leaving Bogotá, we encountered one more life-threatening problem. A problem a million times worse than any of the other life-threatening problems we had experienced the past five days.

As the plane approached the end of the runway, we looked out our windows and saw that we were still on the ground. Panic set in. I already hated flying, and I did not need this.

Obviously the pilot decided that we weren't going to get airborne anytime soon, so he hit the brakes. Crap flew around everywhere, but we stopped. Right at the edge of the runway.

The pilot turned the plane around, made what I guess were some adjustments, and tried again. This time we got up in the air.

I think I lost three years of my life during those three days in Bogotá. Hopefully, since I don't smoke or drink anymore, I can get them back.

The next day we left for Santiago, Chile. And it didn't get any easier.

Guns N' Roses went on two hours late that night, and during the show, specifically during the song "Civil War," bottles were randomly thrown on the stage. No one got hit, and normally Axl would have just left the stage, for fear of getting hit. He had been hit before with objects, as had most of the members of the band. But this night Axl did not leave the stage, probably because he knew something bad would happen. More than

85,000 people were there—the biggest concert ever in that stadium in Santiago.

However, unrelated to the show, something bad did happen. Fifty people were arrested outside the stadium, and through no fault of the band, a teenage fan sustained numerous injuries at the concert and died two days later. Rumor had it that she had snuck out of her house to see the concert, because her parents wouldn't allow her to go.

So sad.

Chilean media reported that Axl was drunk prior to the show. They also reported that drugs were discovered in the band's hotel rooms. This was not even close to true. Axl very rarely drank on the road. He might have had a glass or two of champagne on occasion, but that was it. Axl hardly drank on this entire tour. He was focused on getting his life straightened out.

Plus, both Doug and the manager of the Sheraton San Cristobal hotel denied the accusations.

But officials from the Chilean Department of Investigation came to our hotel floor and checked the rooms for drugs. Luckily nothing was found, but that was a scary moment for all of us on the tour. Specifically, when they were checking my room I kept envisioning that someone would plant drugs in my mattress, and that I would go to jail in Santiago for the rest of my life, and *Midnight Express* came into my mind again. Damn, I hate that movie! I swore the next time a drug search took place in my room, I would be much more prepared.

We left Santiago, unscathed. Next up, Buenos Aires for two shows at the River Plate Stadium.

Believe it or not, nothing happened here. Two great shows went off without any problems. Little did we know that they were just preparing us for when we came back to Buenos Aires in seven months. More on that in a minute.

Next we went to São Paulo, Brazil, for two more shows. Back to the craziness again.

Axl stopped the first show in São Paulo about four times. First, because there was a fight in the crowd. Second, because there were stones being thrown onstage. Third, I think because he got hit with a tennis shoe or something like that. And lastly, during "Paradise City," their final song of the evening, when a stone hit drummer Matt Sorum.

That was the last straw. Axl and the band walked offstage halfway through the song.

I think his parting words that night, were, "Good night, and f*** you, assholes."

The second show in São Paulo was postponed, due to heavy rains. However, Guns N' Roses played the next night with the 120,000 fans in attendance standing in the mud. It was a mess.

Next was the final show of this South American leg in beautiful Rio de Janeiro.

Ah, a nice show. No stress.

Skip ahead to seven months later. The twenty-eight-month tour was almost over. We had just finished the European Skin N' Bones tour, which had us all over Europe for more than two months. We were all tired, and we were all ready to come home.

The last two shows were actually added, as a way for the band to make one last chunk of change before shutting down for a while.

Back to Buenos Aires. Last time we were there nothing strange happened. Just did the two shows and left. But obviously they were gearing up for this one, because this was, by far, the most scared I had ever been on tour with Guns N' Roses.

Before the first of the two shows, we all hung out in our hotel rooms, slowly getting ready. About 70,000 fans were already in the stadium, anticipating the band's arrival. Axl was with Steve, getting his daily adjustment.

At approximately 5 p.m., a group of about fifty police officers from the city's narcotics division descended on the hotel. They were looking for a large amount of cocaine, which had allegedly been stashed in one of the band member's rooms.

They forced their way onto our secure floor and were met by our security team and Doug.

I heard on my walkie-talkie that something was going down, and it didn't sound good. I came out of my hotel room, and there, by the elevators, were a ton of armed policemen talking to Doug and a few others.

I took position in front of Axl's door. At that point he had no idea what was going on. He was eating dinner inside his room, while Steve was taping his ankles for the show.

The chief of police was demanding to see Axl's room. But none of us were telling him which room was Axl's. That was until the guns came out.

Now we were singing like birds. Not really, but this was not funny anymore, this was very serious. Real-life serious.

But before they went in any of the rooms, Doug did something very smart. He negotiated with them that we have an American representative go in the rooms with their team of policemen while the rooms were searched. We were all afraid of drugs being planted in our rooms.

I was prepared. While we waited for the American representative, I ran back into my room and called my mom and dad. From the hotel phone, which cost a small fortune. But I didn't care—I seriously thought my freedom was on the line.

I knew that they would freak out, but it was better than the alternative—having to fly to South America to visit me in prison. I told them what was happening, and that if they didn't hear back from me within the next two hours, I was probably being taken to jail somewhere in Buenos Aires.

I'm a parent now, and I pray I never get that call from any of my kids. My parents were freaking out, but I told them to calm down, and for them to call the police in New York, and the New York press if I didn't call them back in two hours.

I hung up the phone and went back in the hallway.

Eventually the American representative showed up, and the chief of police and his posse started searching the rooms.

Of course, they wanted to start with Axl's room. And because we now had an American representative, we showed them which room was Axl's.

At the same time, down the hall they were searching Robert's room, and they found some of Axl's bath salts in one of his suitcases. Yes, the same bath salts that almost got Robert in trouble in Tel Aviv.

Robert, standing in the hallway dressed only in a bath towel, was now being questioned by police, and he tried to explain to them that they were only bath salts.

They arrived at Axl's hotel room door, and the chief of police knocked. At this point Steve had now heard what was going on in the hallway through his walkie-talkie, so Axl knew as well.

But Steve and Axl didn't answer the door.

"Does anyone have a key?" the chief of police asked.

Damn, I thought to myself. *What do I do now, I do have a key.* I didn't say a thing.

The chief of police yelled through the door.

"Open the door, immediately, or there will be trouble."

There was lots of banter back and forth, but Steve eventually opened the door. The chief of police, the American representative, and about three policemen entered Axl's room. I entered as well, along with Doug. Axl was calmly eating dinner. He allowed them to go through his stuff. He had nothing to hide.

However, there was one problem. The bath salts were also in Axl's room, and I was sure this would give them an excuse to detain him for a few hours.

Then Robert entered the room in his towel, escorted by a policeman; they wanted to test the bath salts.

At the same time, one of the policemen in Axl's bedroom thought he hit the jackpot when he came across about five clear baggies full of more bath salts. More bags of "cocaine," according to the chief of police.

We all tried to explain, very carefully, that they were bags of bath salts.

I forget how they did it, but somehow they ran tests, ran more tests, and finally determined that we were telling the truth.

No cocaine.

After all that, the chief of police and his team were about to leave Axl's room, when the chief turned to Axl and asked for his autograph.

Happened all the time. Give Axl, or members of the band, crap for a few hours, accuse them of something illegal, threaten them, and once nothing is found instantly turn into best friends and expect an autograph.

Incredible.

Axl signed his autograph. Good for him!

All I could think of at that point was, *Damn, they didn't search my room yet, and now they're going to be pissed.*

They came into my room and started searching. Flipping over the mattresses, dumping all my suitcases all over the room, they were determined to find something, anything. All the time though, I watched closely, with my new best friend, the American representative, to see if anyone got any ideas of planting drugs. It was so stressful.

They found nothing.

In two hours they had searched all our rooms and nothing was found.

Axl had Doug and I set up an impromptu press conference and within minutes we had a meeting room, and a room full of reporters, and television crews.

Axl released a live statement of what had just occurred, adding that no drugs were found in any of our rooms. It was fed live to all local television stations.

Only an hour and a half later, Guns N' Roses hit the stage and put on another amazing show.

We found out later that while they were checking our hotel rooms, drug squad officers arrived at the stadium and searched through the band's equipment and instruments as well.

The next night was the last show of the tour. No drug searches, no riots, no one killed. Just one last great show.

And it was now time to say good-bye, until the next tour . . .

But there was no next tour. Not with this group of guys.

No one knew it at the time, but July 17, 1993, would be the last time that this great lineup would play together as members of Guns N' Roses.

I was honored to be there, and to witness a huge part of rock n' roll history.

SLASH "DIES"

There was one night that really stands out in my mind as one of the craziest nights on tour with Guns N' Roses. It easily could have been the saddest, but, thank God, it was not.

It was the night when Slash died for a few minutes.

In a nutshell, Slash apparently met a woman at a party. She provided him with some drugs, bad drugs, and Slash died for a few moments outside my hotel room in the hallway, in San Francisco, California.

I will not elaborate on this story for two reasons. Number one, I did not see it actually happen. All the stories in this book are written because I was there, and it either happened to me, or I witnessed it. I just heard about what happened to Slash later that afternoon. And number two, Slash tells the story very well in his own book *Slash*, so I suggest reading it there.

It was a horrific situation. He basically died from an overdose, they revived him, and I think we played a concert that night or the day after, as if nothing had happened. Truly remarkable.

But what I will add to the existing story is this: That night we had a team meeting—the band and some key members of the entourage, me included. We figured out what we were going to say to everyone else on tour, and we were all sworn to secrecy about what happened that day. The band didn't want the public to know, and this story was buried. At least that's what I thought.

And it was, for a while.

I always thought that someone, somewhere, was going to leak this story, but it just never got out while we were on the road. And if it did, I never saw it, and it never became the lead story it should have become.

When we finished the tour I was asked to do hundreds of interviews on various radio stations and various rock websites around the world. I always turned them down, even though there were times that I was offered money if I had any good juice on the band. It was never even tempting. The band members were my friends.

But one day I was sitting in my house, watching one of those "Behind the Scenes" shows, and they're doing a piece on Guns

N' Roses. I had been asked if I wanted to say something on this show, and I declined, because I knew that they would ask me questions regarding Axl, and I thought it would be boring because I always had "no comment." On the show I see a few people from the entourage being interviewed, and I thought to myself it was cool to see my old buds again. Then I saw John Reese and they're talking to him about the tour, and all of a sudden I heard John telling the story, to the entire world, about the night that Slash died.

I jokingly thought to myself, *Damn, I could have gotten a lot of money for that.*

I found out later that numerous news outlets had already heard about it, but for some reason it was always buried.

Then of course, Slash wrote his book and he went into great detail about that night.

So, I guess it's out there, and now I can say, with a clear conscience, that it's true, Slash's heart did stop one night, right outside my hotel room, in San Francisco, and he lived to tell about it.

Axl looking over the room service menu somewhere in Argentina. Out that window are hundreds, maybe thousands of fans. Robert looks on.

Natasha and me on the MGM Grand airplane.

SHOWS

A TYPICAL SHOW DAY

On a typical show day, I woke up at 9 a.m., for a total of about four hours sleep. I'd light a cigarette, put some dip in my mouth, and while lying in bed, make phone calls to Los Angeles. I'd get ready for that day's gig, as well as advancing the next gig, and I'd order breakfast from room service.

Earl would come in to watch TV. Then Robert would come in to watch TV. So I'd figure, What the hell? I'll watch TV, too. Then Steve, the buff chiropractor, would come in to tell us he's going to the gym. Bastard. I'd put out my cigarette, thinking I would quit and get healthy.

But the phone would ring, and I'd learn something was wrong with, say, the dressing room at the venue for that night. I'd light another cigarette, fix the problem, and move on.

Around noon, Axl would wander in with a menu—he's hungry. He'd tell me what he wants. I'd order his breakfast, and I get a little something for myself. My second breakfast.

Then we'd all sit around and talk about crap—some personal stuff, something about the show last night, and why we're all stuck in this hotel.

The food would arrive, and about 90 percent of the time the waiter noticed Axl sitting on the bed and asked for his autograph. Sometimes Axl gave it, sometimes I told the waiter that we're doing that later. I'd sign for the bill. We'd all eat in my room.

Axl went back to his room to eat if the conversation was about baseball or golf. If it was about football, he stayed. He's an Oakland Raiders fan and I'm a Kansas City Chiefs fan—a perfect match.

After breakfast/second breakfast (if Axl was back in his room) we'd all try to take a nap—each of us somewhere in my room, strategically placed at least ten feet from one another. But as soon as I fell asleep, the phone would ring and I would be presented with another problem. So, I'd light another cigarette, fix the problem, and move on.

At about 5 p.m., Axl would come back and ask what time the show was. Depending on the city, I usually told him a little earlier than scheduled. You all know why. Robert would go to the gig ahead of us to get Axl's clothes and backstage area ready. He'd usually pick out about five or six outfits for Axl to choose from.

Axl would either then meet with his therapist or work out. I'd still be sitting on my bed, eating and waiting for something else to go wrong. Lucky for me, I didn't gain a ton of weight, probably because of the cigarettes I smoked every five minutes, and the dip between my lip and gums.

Axl would then either get adjusted by Steve and/or get a massage from Sabrina. During this time Robert would call me from the venue and tell me that something was missing from Axl's dressing room, either his red bandana or an article of clothing. Or he would share with me the fact that the promoter thought it would be a good idea to replace Axl's bottle of Dom Pérignon with Mumm.

So, I'd light another cigarette, fix the problem, and move on.

About three hours before the show the band and the entourage would head over to the hotel to do sound check. I would stay behind with Steve and Earl, waiting for Axl to get ready. Axl rarely went to sound check.

During sound check I usually received another call informing me that because of the curfew, the time of the show had been moved up an hour and I needed to get Axl to the show as soon as possible. (Yes, there was an actual curfew on many shows—times when the show must end, or they would pull the power.)

So, I'd light another cigarette, fix the problem, and move on.

About an hour before we had to leave for the gig, Axl would jump into the shower and do his vocal warm-ups. After the shower, Steve taped up Axl's ankles. This was because Axl ran around the stage a lot and he wanted to prevent turning an ankle or two—just like the professional ballplayers before a game.

On a good day, we then headed to the hotel lobby, got into the awaiting limo, and went to the gig. But sometimes, because we left so much later than everyone else, we lost track of either the limo driver or the police escort taking us to the venue, and we stood in the lobby scratching our asses.

So, I'd light another cigarette, fix the problem, and move on.

We'd arrive at the gig, Axl popped into his dressing room for a couple of minutes, met with the band for a minute or two, chose the first song, and then ran onto the stage and started the show.

Robert would be stationed at the teleprompter (more on that later) ready for the first song, which had been told to him about five minutes prior. But Axl would get onstage, and it wouldn't be the song they had just changed it to, it would be an entirely different song.

So, I'd light another cigarette, fix the problem, and move on.

But no matter how we got to that point, it always ended up being an amazing show!

A NOT-SO-TYPICAL SHOW DAY

Everything went smooth, we showed up on time, and nothing went wrong during the show.
NEVER HAPPENED!

DIFFERENT SHOW SCHEDULES

There's a rumor out there that Axl Rose is known for being late to shows. I know, hard to believe.

Truth is, Axl was, and still is, late for some shows. I never asked Axl why he's late for his shows, but after living with him 24/7 for about three years I have my own theory and it's quite simple. He wants to put on the best show possible every single night. But to do that he has to get into "the zone," just like they do in sports. You have to get pumped up to put on a show like Axl does, and sometimes, I guess it's just hard to get to that space. Sometimes it took longer than other times, and those were the times he was late.

I can say this for a fact: In all my years with Axl, he never showed up late or canceled a show "just because." There was always a good reason, and I'll just leave it at that.

So, when I took over from Blake I tried to do things a little different, and Axl started showing up on time a lot more than in the past. I'm not saying it was directly me, but I'd like to think I had a small part in it—by bringing a positive attitude to the table every day, and motivating his ass off.

Oh, and I did the following as well . . .

Every day that we had a show, John Reese or Bill Greer slipped a piece of paper under our hotel room doors to tell us what time the sound check was, what time the opening band went onstage, what time Guns N' Roses was supposed to go onstage, and what time curfew was.

The promoters had started getting smart because they knew that GNR was infamous for showing up one to three hours late for shows, so they worked with the cities and began putting curfews on the shows. Truth be known, there was good reason for the curfews. Public transportation stopped at a certain time, so there were many stranded teenagers who couldn't get home safely if a show went too late. I'm sure there were curfews for many other things as well, but GNR was known for testing those time limits.

Here's a typical schedule:

Show Schedule

Doors: 7:30 PM

Brian May: 8:30 PM

Set Change: 9:20 PM

Guns N' Roses: 10:00 PM

Curfew: 12:30 PM

That's what all of us received the morning of a show. This was the *real* schedule. It was said that GNR would be charged $10,000 for every minute they went over the curfew in some cities. Yikes. Now that's motivation. And it worked, because to my knowledge I don't think we ever went over for a long period of time.

But again, I like to think I had a very small hand in it. On certain show days when I thought getting Axl onstage on time would be an issue, I would re-create the show schedule by moving the times up thirty to sixty minutes, and slip it under his door.

So, *my* show schedule for just such a night would read like this:

Doors Open: 7:00 p.m.
Brian May (Opening Act): 8:00 p.m.
Set Change: 8:50 p.m.
Guns N' Roses: 9:30 p.m.
Curfew 12:00 a.m.

Axl would think the show was at 9:30 p.m., so even if he was a little late because of "unforeseen circumstances," we would still be okay.

I'm pretty sure that the schedule that John or Bill put under our doors also had a little buffer in it as well for these reasons, so my extra little buffer was an added insurance policy that the show would finish on time and the band wouldn't get fined.

I never told anyone on the tour that I did this. I didn't have to because I knew that Axl wouldn't discuss show times with anyone else but me. He relied on me to tell him when he had two hours before the show, one hour before the show, when we had to leave, and so on.

No one ever knew I did this . . . until now.

On June 23, 1992, this "curfew thing" was tested.

Axl and Duff weren't feeling too well for a show in Rotterdam, Netherlands, at Feijenoord Stadium. We even had a doctor meet us at the airport to treat Axl so he could do the show that night. But that took extra time.

Guns N' Roses finally went onstage around 10 p.m., about two hours after the warm-up band, Faith No More, finished their set.

Problem was that Feijenoord Stadium had an 11 p.m. curfew. European curfews were much earlier than American curfews. As the deadline approached, the local authorities told the GNR management team that power would be cut at 11:30 p.m. The band was told about the potential dilemma, so Axl announced to the crowd, "You have a right to a complete show. You paid for it. If they cut the power, be my guests, do what you want." With that, there was a meeting of the minds backstage, and the police decided to let the band play on until well after midnight.

No riot that night.

THE DREADED TELEPROMPTER

One of your jobs when you worked for Axl Rose was to run his teleprompter, which had the words to every Guns N' Roses song ever written, as well as the words to some cover songs they performed on a regular basis. Axl wrote the lyrics to many of the songs, but when he was onstage, because there was so much going on, and because he was exerting so much energy, he felt more comfortable if the words scrolled down on a few monitors strategically placed on the stage. This way, if he went off on a tangent, like if he saw a beautiful woman flashing her breasts, he would remember where he was in the song, simply by looking down at the closest monitor.

When I first arrived on the tour, Blake ran the teleprompter. He was great at it. The key to being "great at it," besides knowing the software on those early laptops, was to know all of Guns N' Roses songs after hearing only one or two notes. Experts at the game show *Name That Tune* would have been perfect for this part of the job.

Blake knew all the songs. I didn't.

I knew all their hits, but when I first joined, I didn't know all their other songs. And although I listened to the songs to get up to speed as fast as possible, they sounded much different when they were performed live.

Because it was a thankless job, one of Blake's first goals was to have me run Axl's teleprompter, so he could just sit back and enjoy the show. Yes, there were other things to do during the show, like invite beautiful women backstage, but nothing as stressful as running the teleprompter.

Here's why.

Back in 1991, the home computer was just starting to get popular. I had very minimal experience on a computer at that time. I had one at home, but it ran very slow. The software back then was very basic, and laptops ran even slower. To do the exact job today would be much easier than it was back then.

Before Guns N' Roses hit the stage, the band members had a quick meeting backstage to decide what song they would open with. It was usually "It's So Easy," "Night Train," or once in a while they'd open with "Welcome to the Jungle." Axl or Slash would then tell Blake the opening song, so Blake would have enough time to load it up, and get it ready on the stage monitors. But, after that, it was a free-for-all.

Guns N' Roses did have a set list—a list of songs typed in big print, taped on the floor of the stage at the bottom of all the band members' mic stands. But they hardly ever kept to that list. So when a song was over, either Axl told Slash the next song he wanted to play, or Slash would start playing the next song of his choice. Because Axl was the singer, 99 percent of the time the choice of the song was his, and he would make that decision depending on how his voice felt that night. Blake would have to guess what that song was in a few notes, so he would have time to exit out of the last song, scroll down to the next song (they were

US TOUR SET LIST

NEW	ACOUSTIC
RIGHT NEXT DOOR TO HELL	USED TO LOVE HER
DEAD HORSE	YOUR CRAZY
GARDEN OF EDEN	YOU AIN'T THE FIRST
RECKLESS LIFE	NOVEMBER RAIN
MY MICHELE	PATIENCE
ROCKET QUEEN	**STANDARDS**
DOUBLE TALKIN' JIVE	PARADISE CITY
PERFECT CRIME	WELCOME TO THE JUNGLE
PRETTY TIED UP	SWEET CHILD O' MINE
DON'T CRY	YOU COULD BE MINE
IT'S SO EASY	KNOCKING ON HEAVENS DOOR
NIGHTRAIN	NICE BOYS
YESTERDAYS	CIVIL WAR
ATTITUDE	LIVE & LET DIE
ESTRANGED	**ROTATE BY DATE**
BROWNSTONE	SO FINE
	LOCOMOTIVE
	COMA
	THE GARDEN
	NEW ROSE

A typical Guns N' Roses set list—which was never adhered to.

in alphabetical order), choose that song, then wait for it to load and go live onto the monitors on the stage. But that process took about fifteen seconds, and that's if Blake knew what the song was in the first two seconds.

Luckily most songs have intros, so Blake would usually have between ten and fifteen seconds to get a song up on the monitors. But a song like "Live and Let Die," a Beatles cover, has a one-note intro and then the words start. And we were expected to get the words on the screen that fast.

Impossible.

I sat there every night and marveled at how great Blake was at running the teleprompter, but the thought of running that thing by myself was so overwhelming at first. That's when I think I added dipping to smoking cigarettes.

But it was inevitable. I would take over the teleprompter in a few days.

Leading up to the day it officially became my job, I sat down and did a song or two with Blake loading the song, and me just scrolling down the words as Axl sang. As time went on, I did more songs, and Blake started to step away. I'd run a song, and the song would be about to end, so I would turn around to make sure Blake was there, and sometimes he wasn't, and I'd start to sweat, and then he would appear, to save the day.

Well, the dreaded day to run the teleprompter by myself came. I was stressed, but I had a plan.

Slash had become a good friend of mine on the road. I went drinking with him, and kept up, oh, maybe for the first fifteen minutes, and then he drank me under the table.

The teleprompter room was located on the stage, under the stage-left ramp, right next to Axl's onstage dressing room, and directly stage-left of where Slash stands onstage. So because Slash was my bud, and because he was standing only four feet away from me for 75 percent of the concert, I asked Slash to help me out with the songs until I got comfortable with them. I asked him to yell the next song to me through my tiny twelve-by-twelve-inch hole as soon as he knew what it was, and I would bring it up on the stage monitors.

He agreed. Bless his heart.

But then I found out soon thereafter that Slash loves a good prank now and then.

Earl had been on the road for a while and he knew the songs well, so as a backup, I asked him to also shout the name of the next song to me.

So, I was set. I had everything in place for the big night.

The first song was easy because they told me what it was before they hit the stage.

One down, about twenty-four to go. Ugh.

The second song that night was "Welcome to the Jungle." It has a long-ass intro so even if I had made a mistake, I could have corrected it before Axl started singing. I got that one.

I thought to myself, *This is going to be okay.*

Next few songs were all good as well. Slash wasn't yelling them out to me, because they were playing all their hits and I guess he assumed that I knew them. I didn't even have to turn to Earl, because I knew all the songs.

But then it happened—an intro I had never heard before.

Panic. I immediately calmed down because I knew Slash would be there for me. And on cue, there he was. His face appeared in my little cut-out window, and he said, "Used to Love Her."

So I brought up "Used to Love Her," even as I thought to myself, *I kinda know this song, and it doesn't sound like this.* But I trusted Slash.

I clicked on the LAST button to make the song go live to the monitors onstage, and there it was in all its glory: "Used to Love Her" on the monitors.

Phew. Disaster averted.

Axl started singing, and I looked at the screen on my laptop, and I noticed that Axl's not singing the words on my screen, or more importantly on the screen he would probably look at in the next few seconds.

I stuck my head out of my little window and saw Slash cracking up onstage. He just looked at me and smiled.

"Oh crap!" I yelled.

I started looking around, while remaining seated, trying to find someone to help me. Earl shrugged his shoulders because he didn't know the song. But he had a smirk on his face as well. I knew where this was going.

Then Axl looked down at the monitor, and you could see immediately the confusion and anger on his face.

He whipped his head around and stared me down from about twenty feet away.

I pressed a few buttons and took the song off the screen. Axl was now staring at a blank screen.

Luckily he still remembered the words to the song and kept singing, and even luckier, it was a duet with Duff. Every once in a while Axl would look down at the monitor to see if I had figured out the song yet.

Nothing.

And little did I know, Duff had a monitor in front of him, as well, also with a blank screen.

I remembered thinking that Duff would probably like the words to the song up there as well. I was going to have two people pissed at me after the show.

I decided to wait until the chorus of the song came, and get the words up in time for the second verse. But there was no definitive chorus.

I went the entire song without putting up the words.

Then, I started thinking how I was going to get home after I got fired. Would they pay for my flight, or would I have to pay for it? The name of the song that night was "So Fine."

I never missed that song again.

The rest of the night went pretty smooth, and it got easier and easier the more I did it. Once in a while Slash would give me the correct song, and once in a while he'd try to mess me up. But when Blake left I knew I had to get another assistant so I could get rid of this responsibility.

And I did just that.

Me running Axl's teleprompter.

"YOU'RE FIRED"

The joke on the road was that if you were the sound-monitor guy, your job would last about a week. I don't know much about this because the monitor guy was in the crew, and while I knew most of them I didn't have time to hang with them because I was with Axl and/or the entourage. But during the show I was near the monitor guy, and it seemed there would be a new one every month or so. Maybe some were fired because they couldn't get the mix right onstage, or maybe some quit because they weren't able to please the band because they couldn't get the mix correct onstage.

I was also fired one night by Axl.

Axl and I were very close on the road. We basically lived with each other 24/7 for at least three years. I knew *everything* about him, and he knew *everything* about me. Yes, he was my boss, but we became very good friends, and remain friends to this day.

But in the heat of the moment, in the heat of a concert in front of 80,000 people, things can go wrong and someone has to take the blame.

And one night it was me.

Axl lost his place in a song. I think it was "You Could Be Mine."

I had the song up on his teleprompter, and everything was going smoothly. He sang the first verse and the chorus.

I scrolled down. All good.

But all of a sudden he started singing the first verse of the song again, and because it probably didn't feel right to him, he looked down at the monitor, and saw that I had completely different words on the screen than what he was singing. I was in the second verse. So, he continued singing the first-verse words, throwing in a few words of the second verse just because.

He became totally confused.

While he was singing, in full view of the crowd, he peeked into my little window, and said, "What verse are we in?"

I said, "Second verse, just do those words on the screen."

"I just sang those words."

"No, I'm pretty sure you sang the first verse twice."

And with that, in the heat of the moment, he said, "Screw you, you're fired."

Up to that point Axl had never gotten mad at me. He got pissed at other people for things that went wrong, but he had never been pissed at me.

Apparently, I skipped right over pissed, and went right into FIRED mode.

So I left. At that point there was no one to run the teleprompter, and I knew that. Blake had already left, and I didn't have another assistant yet. So for the rest of the concert that night there was no teleprompter. And the show went great, from what I heard.

I was pissed because I knew that I hadn't done anything wrong. But Doug told me to go back to the hotel, and that it would all blow over.

I went back to the hotel and watched television.

To be honest, I was relieved for a while. The stress level on a tour like that takes its toll, and sometimes you needed a break.

So I just hung back in the room while everyone else was at the show, ordered room service, watched a movie, and relaxed.

It was awesome.

But I knew that Axl and I would talk, and I knew in my heart that everything would be fine.

And it was. Axl apologized for going off on me, I apologized for being right. We laughed and it was all good.

A few weeks later I hired another assistant, my best friend from California, Robert Finkelstein.

I had met Robert years before. We both worked as waiters at Hamburger Hamlet on Sunset Boulevard in Hollywood.

I called him up and offered him the job and, of course, he was ecstatic. It's not every day that you get a phone call where you're asked to tour with one of the biggest bands in the history of rock.

I immediately told Robert that one of the jobs he needed to do right away was to run Axl's teleprompter during the show. I told him it was easy, and that it would be the least stressful part of his day. He was all excited.

I told him to go out and buy every Guns N' Roses CD, and to listen to all their songs, and to memorize them.

And he did.

But the first night he saw what I did on the teleprompter, he freaked out, just like I did, and he wanted no part of it. I told him that this was his gig, and that he had to do it. Now he was stressed, and I was going to be less stressed.

And that was good for me. Pay your dues, right?

So Robert took over the teleprompter position after about two weeks of training.

But just like it happened to me, Robert was fired one night for something to do with Axl's clothes onstage, and I thought that I would have to run the teleprompter again.

After Robert was fired, John Reese felt that because Axl was so pissed that it would be a good idea for Robert to check into another hotel before he was sent home the next day.

But again, Axl was over it immediately after the show, and he asked me, "Where's Robert?"

I told Axl that John had gotten Robert a room in another hotel, and that Robert thought he was being sent home the next day.

Tom Mayhue, Axl's personal "roadie" and onstage technician, was in the dressing room with Axl and me. Tom was known for loving to play pranks on people, and decided that this would be a great opportunity.

Axl agreed.

And the "fun" began.

Tom called Robert and proceeded to tell him how pissed off Axl was, and that he has never seen Axl this pissed before, and that we're going to be back in the hotel in five minutes, and that Axl is going to go off on him.

Robert hadn't even started packing yet, and he didn't know what hotel John was sending him to.

This went on for about fifteen minutes. Relentless.

And that's what the tour was like. You had to be thick-skinned, or you'd be eaten up and spit out on a daily basis.

Tom let Robert off the hook, and Robert was welcomed back with open arms. Robert ended up finishing out the tour with me, and we both worked for Axl after the tour was over.

THE BANANA SPLIT THING

It wasn't just Tom, everyone on the road loved to play pranks on each other, so I figured I would take my turn with Robert. I mean, what are friends for, right?

Remember, we all lived together twenty-four hours a day, seven days a week, so we were all really tight, and when a new person came along everyone was "on alert." But since Robert was my friend he didn't have it so bad with the rest of the entourage. It was just me he was really worried about.

One of the things I told Robert about was the so-called initiation process. I told Robert that whenever a new person joined the Guns N' Roses entourage, there would be a time when he would have to deal with the "banana split thing."

Of course Robert asked, "What the heck is the banana split thing?"

I told him, "At some point the band or the crew is going to tackle you backstage, or on the side of the stage, and they're going to tie you up, and they're going to bring you onstage, and in front of 80,000 people they're going to take your pants down and they're going to make a banana split in your ass."

No response.

So I said, "I know, it's horrible, but at least you get to tour with Guns N' Roses, right?"

Robert came alive and said, "Dude, you're not going to let them do that to me, right? Did they do it to you?"

"Not yet. But, I think it's because Blake left, and they didn't want to risk losing me if I freaked out, so I think I got lucky. But everyone else pretty much had it done to them."

Again, no response. Just sheer terror in my poor buddy's face.

Now, most people would have let their friend off the hook by now, but not me. Not after I saw the fear on his face. It was just too good.

So I went back to doing what I was doing and added, "Don't worry, maybe they'll forget about it, and it won't happen to you." And I went back into my hotel room.

I looked through my hotel room door peephole and saw Robert run into his room, I'm sure with his butt-cheeks fully clenched.

I milked this for the next few days, telling Robert things like, "I think I heard one of the guys say 'banana split tonight,' or 'Axl wants me to buy vanilla ice cream,' and that's weird because I know he hates vanilla ice cream."

Evil, I know.

After a few more days I actually went to the grocery store and bought a bunch of bananas, and had one of the guys in the entourage walk through the hotel lobby carrying a grocery bag with the bananas sticking out of the top, calling over to Robert to say, "Hi," while Robert was at the hotel's front desk. Robert saw the bag and the bananas and, I assume, went into internal panic mode.

Later that afternoon, Robert sat at the lobby bar, probably trying to get drunk to dull the pain of what he thought was going to happen that night. Another member of our entourage sat next to him and started taking the cherries from the bar and putting them in a plastic bag.

Classic.

Robert just got up and left. The timing was perfect. Robert was freaking out because there was a show that night.

Robert was very elusive at the concert that night, looking behind him every second, and on edge every time someone walked near him.

But Robert also knew that he had to be on the side of the stage during the show, because he had to be near me, just in case I needed his help.

So at the show, guys from the entourage would convene around Robert, as if something was about to happen. Robert would either run away to the other side of the stage, or run backstage as if he had to get something for Axl. It was a very stressful night for Robert, and a very hysterical night for us.

But nothing happened that night. In fact nothing happened for a long time, but every once in a while we would allude that "it was going to happen tonight."

Until . . .

PRETTY TIED UP

We were in Italy on Wednesday, June 30, 1993, coming to the end of the tour. Only a few months left. My wedding date was in September, and at that point I was really tired of traveling to a different city every other day. I think we all were.

It was the Skin N' Bones part of the world tour, where during the middle of the set, the band paused the show, and the crew brought out a couch, a few comfy chairs, and a lamp or two, creating a living-room kind of feel. It was all brought onstage, right onto the apron where the front row was only about ten feet away from the entire band.

From the couches and the chairs, Guns N' Roses then performed a small acoustic set—songs like "Patience," "Used to Love Her," and so on.

That night, because it was near the end of the tour, and we were all mentally fried, it was time to do something different at the show. Something really fun. Something outside the box. So we decided to tie up Robert and bring him onto the stage, right in the middle of a song.

We took a real chance with this because we didn't tell the band that this was going to happen. But we knew the band loved practical jokes, and we thought they'd be okay with it. Plus, there was only a month left on the tour, and if they fired the four of us at that point, it would take them a month, at least, to find replacements, and we were overseas. We knew we were safe, which made it a lot more fun.

The whole banana split joke never happened, and everyone had forgotten about it. Even Robert. But when we decided to tie Robert up, I also decided that I would tell him that while it might have taken awhile, we never forgot the banana split initiation.

I told Robert that I would run the teleprompter that night, and he was really happy about that. But, again, he still had to be stationed next to me just in case Axl or I needed him to do something, because I couldn't leave the teleprompter.

The band was playing "Used to Love Her," and we had decided that that would be our cue. We chose that song because it wasn't a major hit song, and it was a fun song. I know you wouldn't know it from the title or the lyrics ("I used to love her, but I had to kill her"), but from the stage it's a very fun song, and Axl seemed to enjoy "playing" during it. So we figured, if we're going to dump someone on the stage in the middle of a song in front of 80,000 people, the band better be having fun, or we'd be in serious trouble.

Earl was usually stationed in Axl's onstage dressing room, but it wasn't out of the ordinary for him to come out to say hi to me or Robert. Doug and John usually hung around the area behind me as well.

I did not witness this part, but I assume that Earl engaged Robert in a discussion while Truck and Ronnie (Slash's security guy) came over from their side of the stage to get ready to pounce. Everyone was in place as Robert stood enjoying the show, not knowing what was about to take place.

Andy Warhol once said that everyone, at one time or another, will get their fifteen minutes of fame—fifteen minutes where you are the star, the center of attention. Although Robert was an actor who had appeared on a few television shows and onstage, being in front of 80,000 people live was going to be something new for him. It would be something he would never forget.

And neither would we.

About a quarter of the way into "Used to Love Her," it happened. Poor Robert, poor innocent Robert, who was standing on the side of the stage, minding his own business, enjoying the show he had seen a hundred times, was jumped by four huge men, each from different angles.

Because I was running the teleprompter, I couldn't get up to help, but it happened literally two feet behind me.

It was Earl, Truck, Ronnie, and I think John was in there, too. They brought Robert to the ground, gently. Well, as gently as four very large men can bring someone down.

At that point Robert wasn't putting up too much of a fight. He probably needed a second or two to comprehend what was happening, and since he had no idea of what was *about* to happen, he didn't feel he had anything to panic about.

That was until I spoke.

"Looks like it's banana split night, Robert."

And Robert went crazy. He started swinging his arms and kicking his legs, desperately trying to break the hold of four very strong men.

It's amazing what adrenaline can do. Robert suddenly had the strength of ten men.

Robert was always in great shape. But if I had to guess he probably topped out at about 180 pounds. And although he worked out, what I witnessed was truly superhuman strength.

The four guys had him held pretty well, but the idea was that two of them would hold him down, and the other two would tie his legs together, and tie his hands behind his back.

That wasn't going to happen. All four were needed just to hold him down. As soon as one of the four let go for a second, Robert was able to wriggle away. This went on for about two minutes, which just so you know, is an eternity when you're trying to tie someone up.

I had to scrap the teleprompter for a few seconds to help out. Axl knew this song inside and out, so I figured he could wing it with the words for a minute or two.

I jumped in to help my four huge friends hold down the 180-pound ex-actor, and we were finally able to tie him up.

We were all sweating profusely. Robert laid on the ground all tied up, catching his breath as well.

But we weren't finished yet.

Earl grabbed one end, Ronnie grabbed the other, and they lifted Robert up. At that point there was nothing Robert could do, and he had no energy left, so there was no struggle when they lifted him up.

While the band was in the middle of their song, and Axl was singing his heart out, Earl and Ronnie carried Robert onstage.

The band continued to play while this happened, but they were cracking up.

Earl and Ronnie carried Robert right in front of Axl, right on the edge of the front of the stage. They placed him down and left. Robert lay there, the band continued to play, and Axl continued to sing.

And there began Robert's fifteen minutes of fame, onstage with Guns N' Roses, in front of 80,000 screaming fans.

After a minute or two of watching Robert try to break free from the ropes, Axl decided to take it to the next level. While singing, Axl started hopping back and forth over Robert as if jumping rope.

On the side of the stage we were all relieved because we knew we wouldn't get fired. By the way things looked onstage, we thought we might actually get raises.

The band finished the song, and Axl didn't tell us to get Robert. Instead they broke into their next song, and left him there.

During this song Axl put the microphone in front of Robert during parts of the chorus so Robert could sing along. Think of it. Yes, Robert was still trying to get loose because he still thought that he was going to get a banana shoved up his ass, but he's singing a duet with Axl Rose. This was a story he could tell for generations.

This continued for a few more songs, all the time Robert wriggling around trying to get loose. Every once in a while, Axl would grab a towel from the stage and wipe Robert's brow because he was sweating so much. And every once in a while Axl would notice that Robert was loosening the ropes and have one of the guys come back onstage to tighten the knot.

It was brutal, but it was one of the funniest fifteen minutes I have ever experienced in my life.

The band started yet another song, and again, Robert was left out there. About halfway through the song, though, Axl looked at Robert and stopped the song.

"Hold it, hold it," Axl yelled in his mic for everyone to hear.

The band stopped playing.

"He's got a knife," Axl added.

Robert had managed to get one of his hands into his front pocket, pull out a small pocket knife, and slowly cut the thick rope. Axl was so into Robert being onstage that he called Earl and had him take the knife away from Robert.

Then, the band picked up the song right where they left off.

At that point Robert must have thought that this was never going to end, and the fight in him left, like a fish out of water.

It actually looked like Robert started enjoying the experience because I think he realized that there would be no banana split that night.

In fact, no one had ever had the banana split.

Robert was eventually released, and lived to tell the story of his fifteen minutes of fame with Guns N' Roses in Italy.

It might have been hell that night, but today it's one hell of a story.

THE DOMINO'S PIZZA GUY

Imagine this. You get a call to deliver a pizza and the address happens to be backstage at the local concert arena, and you deliver the pizza. The next thing you know you're playing bongos onstage with Guns N' Roses.

The acoustic set during the Skin N' Bones tour was unique, and it happened to be one of my favorite parts of the tour. Slash played acoustic guitar, and Matt played bongos instead of his usual drum set.

Stage pranks were a recurring theme on tour. I'm not sure who started this, but I'm guessing it was either Doug or Dale "Opie" Skeirseth, the production manager. Opie was basically in charge of the stage, the crew, and the equipment. He ran the whole show.

One night someone ordered a bunch of pizza from Domino's and had it delivered backstage of an arena. On this night the Domino's deliveryman arrived backstage, and someone instructed him to take the pizza out to Axl, who was in the middle of performing a song. And much to Axl's credit, he did what every red-blooded rock star would do. He stopped the song, took the box of pizza, placed it on the cocktail table, took a slice out, and started eating it. And so the rest of the band joined in for a slice of pizza.

The face on the Domino's deliveryman was priceless. I think he was in shock. He stood there frozen in front of about 18,000 screaming fans.

With that, Axl walked the Domino's pizza guy over to the bongos, and told him to play the bongos during their next song. Matt grabbed the cymbals or maracas and played those.

Without missing a beat they went into "Used to Love Her," and there he was in all his glory, the Domino's pizza guy playing bongos onstage with the biggest rock band in the world at the time.

I would love to know what that kid is doing now. So if you're out there, Domino's pizza guy, please contact me. I want you to play bongos at my next RockStar Marketing BootCamp seminar in Los Angeles where I teach regular businesspeople how to become "RockStars" in their industry. www.CraigDuswalt.com.

After the song, the pizza guy left the stage to a standing ovation. But one of our guys made sure to "buy" his Domino's shirt, because we were going to use that for the rest of the Skin N' Bones Tour.

I'm sure he had a lot of explaining to do to his boss when he got back to the store without a shirt. But I'm also sure when the boss heard the reason he didn't have his shirt anymore, he was the talk of the town.

For most of the rest of the shows in the Skin N' Bones tour, the band did something really cool. They would choose someone from either the crew or the entourage to come onstage, wearing the Domino's pizza shirt, to play bongos with the band. The audience thought it was a pizza delivery guy, but it was just one of us.

I was blessed to play bongos during the second-to-last show of the tour in Buenos Aires.

I think there were about 80,000 people in the audience that day, and there I was, playing "Used to Love Her" with Guns N' Roses.

There is no feeling in the world that compares to playing a song in front of that many people. This is the reason that just about everyone in the world, at one time or another, wants to be a rock star.

JAMES ON FIRE

I am married to Natasha because James Hetfield, the lead singer/guitarist of Metallica, stood on top of a flash pot during their set and suffered second-degree burns on his arms and hands on August 8, 1994, in Montreal, Canada.

On one of the legs of the Guns N' Roses World Tour was a three-month stint when Guns N' Roses and Metallica shared the stage in large stadiums all across North America. We played Arrowhead Stadium (my favorite, being a Chiefs fan), Giants Stadium, Texas Stadium, the Superdome in Louisiana, and the Houston Astrodome just to name a few. I had personally never seen anything like it.

The lineup that night in Montreal was Faith No More, then Metallica, and then Guns N' Roses closing the show.

Everything started out great. Faith No More's set was awesome, and Metallica took the stage pretty much on time.

But about sixty minutes into Metallica's set, something went horribly wrong.

Apparently the band members of Metallica were warned about some new pyrotechnic cues before they took the stage that night. Obviously there was some miscommunication, because during the song "Fade to Black," James was caught in the middle of a stream of flames that left his left arm badly burned. Metallica had to stop their show.

Because Metallica's set had ended about sixty to ninety minutes early, the crowd had to wait longer than normal for Guns N' Roses to take the stage.

About two hours later Guns N' Roses took the stage, and the crowd went nuts. It was a great beginning of the set.

But something was just "off" that night. Obviously everyone was concerned about James and his injury, but also Axl had been experiencing throat issues for a few weeks before this show.

In my opinion, Axl trashed his voice every night because he put everything into his shows. He screamed and hit some pretty high notes on a consistent basis. No matter how much he warmed up, his songs were very difficult to sing live a few nights a week. Now, as a professional speaker, especially during the three- to five-day events when I speak for ten to twelve hours a day, I expect to lose my voice for a few days. So I can sympathize with Axl. It takes a toll after a while.

That night in Montreal, I think Axl hit the wall. About fifty-five minutes into the set, Axl just walked off the stage. Unfortunately it happened the same night that something happened to James, but I was there, and I truly feel it was just a coincidence. One incident had nothing to do with the other.

Well, the crowd got pissed because they felt like they didn't get an entire show, and about one or two thousand fans took their aggressions out on the stadium seats and the stores, and they smashed windows and set fires.

That night is now known as the Montreal Riot.

There was the previous St. Louis Riot, which I was not there for, but every music fan pretty much knows what happened there.

So this was now riot number two.

While we were backstage we were informed that a riot was starting in the concourse, and that we should leave the stadium immediately.

We did.

Within hours it was all over every news program. MTV had updates every hour on the hour. GNR was getting some really bad press. And to make matters worse, the next two weeks of the tour were canceled while we waited for James's wounds to heal.

So the band went back to Los Angeles for a much-needed rest. Everyone except Axl, Earl, Robert, and me. Axl decided he wanted to fly to New York to visit his girlfriend, Victoria's Secret model Stephanie Seymour. I was really happy because I would get to pay my family an unexpected visit.

Little did I know, this little jaunt to New York would literally change my life.

I booked the four of us in a hotel in New York City, and Axl was happy just hanging in the hotel with Stephanie, and since Earl was there, I was free to go visit friends and hang with family.

The first night, Robert and I went to the Hard Rock Café, and I met some other friends there. The next night, Air Supply happened to be playing the Westbury Music Fair in Long Island—the exact place where Air Supply took me away from my job nine years prior. I decided to go to the concert. I brought some family and friends and we had an awesome time.

After the show I headed backstage to say hi to my great friends Russell Hitchcock and Graham Russell of Air Supply. There I saw another very dear friend of mine, Beth Thompson. We started talking and I asked her if she ever saw her friend Natasha anymore. A year before, on August 14, 1991, my sister, Pamela, who was on the "modeling circuit" with Beth and Natasha, had set me up on a blind date with Natasha.

Pamela had told Natasha, "You have to meet my brother." Natasha's "dork alert radar" must have gone up immediately. She probably thought, *Someone's brother? Yuck.* Natasha lived in Los Angeles, but she frequently flew to New York to do shows, and she worked with Beth and Pamela consistently. They had all become very good friends. So because they were close, Natasha had agreed to go to lunch with me.

Our date was really awesome. Natasha was beautiful and really funny. But back then I was still kind of seeing someone, and she had told me about a guy living in a Dumpster outside her apartment, and that he was stalking her. I really didn't want to "get involved." And although I had really liked her, I was still going to be on tour for at least another eight months, so I thought it best to just become friends. Natasha had felt the same way.

So it was a year later at the Air Supply concert, and I asked Beth about Natasha, and she said, "That's so weird, she's staying with me in my apartment."

I got Natasha's new phone number.

Axl, Earl, Robert, and I stayed in New York one more day and then we headed back to Los Angeles.

When we stayed in Los Angeles for a while, Axl stayed at his home in Malibu and the band put me up at a hotel in Los Angeles. This particular time I was staying at Le Parc Suite Hotel in Hollywood, an awesome boutique hotel that housed numerous rock stars over the years.

I got settled in, and while lying out in the sun at the rooftop pool I decided to call Natasha and see what she was doing. For some reason I was nervous to make the call, but I did. She wasn't home, so I left a message.

That night she called me back. I told her that I was unexpectedly in town and asked her if she wanted to go to dinner. She agreed.

The next night, August 14, 1992, exactly one year after our blind date, we went on our second date at Tommy Tang's Restaurant on Melrose Boulevard.

We sat outside on the back patio and had a very romantic dinner. To lighten the mood, I talked about a guy I had met in Las Vegas (see the UFO Nick story later in this book), and I told her how he was able to move alien spaceships by pointing to them in space and moving his finger. Natasha thought I was giving her the "dumb blonde" test, and she almost climbed out of the bathroom window to get away from me.

Almost.

But she didn't leave, because besides the awful UFO Nick part of the dinner, we fell in love that night.

Six weeks later we got engaged, and less than a year later, Natasha became my wife, and still is to this day, and will be forever. We are truly soul mates.

But here's the really cool and amazing part of this entire adventure. I wasn't supposed to be in New York that night, and I wasn't supposed to go to the Air Supply concert and see Beth. I was supposed to be on tour with Guns N' Roses traveling through Canada, doing more shows with GNR and Metallica.

Natasha was modeling in New York. But she was booked to fly from New York to Chicago to model another line of bathing suits for another manufacturer. But unlike every other time in the past, Natasha decided to cancel going to Chicago, and decided to fly home to Los Angeles instead.

She had no reason for it, except that she felt compelled to come home.

Natasha has always had amazing instincts. There was an incident where she sat in a restaurant at a table next to a full-length window, and after about five minutes decided to move her seat because she "felt something." Two minutes later a car smashed through the window and destroyed the table she was just sitting at moments earlier. So when her instinct told her not to fly to Chicago, she canceled her gig, and flew home.

Neither of us was supposed to be in Los Angeles on August 14, 1992. But we were, and we had dinner. And we fell in love.

Oh, and one more thing. The night I was at the Hard Rock Café in New York City, I was at the downstairs bar. That same night, that same time, Natasha was also at the same Hard Rock Café, sitting at a table upstairs.

So, we owe everything to James Hetfield's unfortunate incident and Axl Rose's desire to go to New York that night.

Sometimes, things are just meant to be.

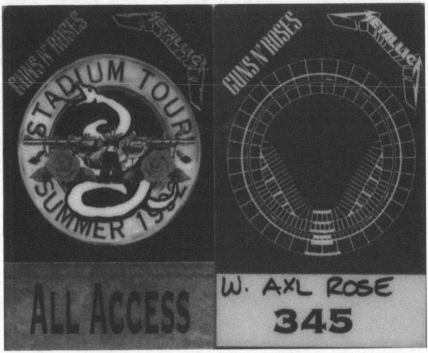

Axl's all-access pass. He never wore it, so I wore his as well as mine.

Me, Steve Thaxton (Axl's chiropractor), and Duff backstage.

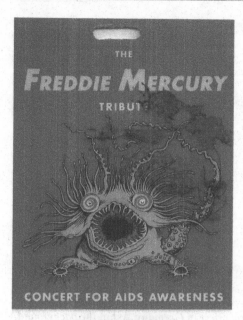

ARTIST
4

My all-access pass for the Freddie Mercury Tribute Concert at Wembly Stadium in London, England.

Robert Finkelstein and me on tour.

Robert, me, and Natasha at an Oktoberfest in Germany. Axl in the background.

SUNDAY
GUNS N' ROSES

ALL THE NEWS THAT'S FIT TO PRINT

TODAY'S DATE *JANUARY 31*

WAKEUP ———— 11 30 AM
LUGGAGE ———— 12 NOON
LIMOS/VANS ———— 2 30 PM
FLIGHT TO MELBOURNE ——— 4 00 PM

REASON FOR EARLY FLIGHT
CREW HAS TO SET-UP SHOW
MONDAY 2/1
SHOW IN MELBOURNE

*These notes would be slipped under our doors every
day, providing us with the schedule for the day.*

FANS

WHERE DO I APPLY?

One of the most interesting questions I got
asked on the road was, "How do I get a job
like yours?"

I didn't really get to "hang" with fans on
the road because all of my time was spent
with Axl, so if I heard the question it was usually yelled to me from a sea of fans as Axl and
I were getting into a limo or going into a restaurant.

Most of the time I would just ignore the question because we
were always in a hurry.

But one night, I think it was in Vancouver, Canada, I was walking out of a hotel by myself, and this guy, maybe twenty-eight
years old, came up to me and said, "Hey, dude, I want to do what
you do. Can you get me an application?"

I started laughing. "An application? Are you serious?"

The guy said, "Yeah, I could do what you do."

He was right. He probably could. It wasn't rocket science. But
one thing I knew for sure—he wasn't getting my job.

So I decided to have a little fun.

I called him aside, and I told him not to share this info with anyone—made it sound very secret. I told him to nonchalantly walk over to the elevator and to go to Room 907. I added that there would be a lady there, and for him to ask her for an application, and that Craig Duswalt sent you.

He beamed.

I reiterated, "Do not tell anyone else. We only do this for special people."

He said thanks and ran to the hotel elevator.

I jumped into the waiting limo and told the driver to go quickly. I did not want to be around when he came back downstairs.

Not only did I not know anyone in 907, I'm pretty sure there wasn't even a Room 907, considering the hotel was only about five or six stories high. I know, I know—I'm awful. But on the road, you'll do anything to keep yourself amused.

If the person I did that to is reading this book, I guess I'm sorry. But that's what you get for asking a STUPID QUESTION.

As we all know, there is no application for that kind of job. It's the ultimate "who you know" gig. Or, you have to be extremely lucky. I was in the right place at the right time with Air Supply. But, as I say at all my seminars: Always do your best, always be positive, and never whine, because you never know who's watching.

That is how I got the gig with GNR.

AUTOGRAPHS

As I mentioned earlier, I was an actor for a while and my "big break" came when I landed a small role as a waiter on the soap opera *General Hospital* on and off for about a year. Never said much, basically just walked around in Duke's Club carrying a tray with drinks. Once in a while I would say, "Here you go," and I would get extra money for that. In the industry when you say a line or two you get more money because you're then considered an "Under 5" (a soap opera actor who has under five lines of dialogue in an episode).

When I was on tour with GNR I knew no one would recognize me from *General Hospital*, so I knew I'd never sign autographs.

How wrong I was.

I found myself signing autographs. Not a ton, but a few here and there. However I wasn't signing my own name. I signed emergency autographs with Axl's name. Bottom line: Axl was very busy on the tour and he didn't have a lot of extra time to sign an autograph at a moment's notice. He had tons of other things on his mind. So, if I needed something quick, or if I had to get someone out of trouble, I would say, can I get you an autographed picture of Axl? Would that make you happy?

Of course they would always agree. If Axl was available, I would walk in my room, grab an 8 × 10 of Axl and a black Sharpie, walk into Axl's room, ask him to sign an autograph, and give it to the person. But if, say, Axl was in the shower, I felt that might be inappropriate, so I would grab the 8 × 10, grab the black Sharpie, sign Axl's name, and give it to the person. It looked exactly the same. In fact, I think my autograph looked better than his.

But just to make it clear, here's my disclaimer: Axl did sign tons of autographs himself as well. And he *always* signed autographs himself if it was for a sick child, a loyal fan, and/or a very special occasion.

BACKSTAGE

We've all heard the stories about what goes on backstage after a rock concert. Many stories have been documented in books written by people way more famous than me. So, I am here to share some of the things that went on backstage after a Guns N' Roses concert.

First of all there was not only one backstage room. With Guns N' Roses, we sometimes had three rooms, or three backstage areas. One room for the radio show winners, one room for family and friends, and one room for the "talent."

Apart from that, Axl had his own dressing room, and the rest of the band shared a really large dressing room.

There were other rooms for the crew as well.

The room with the radio show winners was for exactly that. Local radio shows worked with promoters and gave away free tickets in exchange for ads promoting the concert and/or some free on-air press. The free tickets to the show usually included backstage passes. As part of the contract one, sometimes two, of the band members were required to go into this room after the concert and take pictures with the winners and sign auto-graphs. In all my time with Guns N' Roses, I don't remember Axl ever stepping foot in that room. I don't know why, but I have my theories. I think the main reason Axl didn't go into that room was probably because after a show he rested for a few minutes, and then jumped into the shower to warm down his voice with vocal exercises. If he had to speak to a room full of people after singing his butt off for two hours, he would lose his voice more often.

The second backstage room was for family and friends. When there are more than 150 people in the band, entourage, and crew, chances are that someone is going to have family or a bunch of friends living in the city the band is playing.

We were all allotted a certain amount of comp tickets and a few backstage passes to give away to family and friends. The bigger cities, like New York, Los Angeles, Dallas, Chicago, Miami, and San

Francisco, were all tough to get comp tickets and backstage passes. And me, being from New York, it was tough to get tickets for *all* my friends and family. I always said, if I lived in Iowa, I could have gotten tickets for all my friends and my entire extended family. But New York was tough, especially because the record company also had their people who needed tickets and backstage passes.

This backstage area was for all these VIPs. The room was filled with drinks and food for everyone. This is where I hung out the most, especially after I started dating Natasha, because you could really get in trouble in the third room.

Ah, the third room—the room with all the "talent."

"Talent" was the term for all the beautiful women plucked out of the audience during the show. It was amazing how great our staff was in their ability to find all these beautiful women.

During one part of the tour, Stuart Bailey, Axl's brother, was in charge of putting together the backstage party in the talent room. He put together theme parties and they were quite amazing. I remember there was a Vegas night where he had shipped in blackjack tables, craps tables, and dealers as well. I heard numbers flying around, and I do not know that this is a fact, but I heard that Stuart's budget for these types of backstage parties was in the $100,000 per night range.

Unfortunately, or fortunately, depending on your point of view, that didn't last too long.

But on the nights that $100,000 wasn't spent on the room's décor and theme, it was still the most popular room after a show. For it was not uncommon for people to misplace their clothing in this room, for people to get drunk in this room, for events to take place in this room that I will take to the grave because I'm just not part of the scene anymore.

But imagine what you think might go on backstage after a Guns N' Roses concert, and multiply it by, oh, let's just say ten, conservatively, and you'd still be short.

Here's an example . . .

Indianapolis, Indiana.

Outside of Axl's dressing room, maybe down the hall a little bit, there was parked an Indianapolis 500 race car. A real, authentic car that ran in the Indianapolis 500. We all got to sit in it before the show. Very cool.

After the show, the car was still there, yet something about the car was different this time.

Sitting on top of the car was one of the fans that someone invited backstage. She was a beautiful, petite girl, probably about twenty-three years old. And she was obviously a little tipsy. And she was also stark naked.

Although nudity is a common occurrence backstage, this was quite different. She was making love to the car. I'm not talking about caressing the car with her hands and kissing the side view mirrors. I'm talking about a full-on grind, complete with *ahhs*, and *ooohs*, and a couple of, "oh yeah, faster . . ."

No one told her to do this, no one was egging her on, she just felt compelled, I guess, to do this to the car. A crowd formed around the car, both men and women just staring in amazement. This went on for a few minutes until she had what appeared to be a full-on, honest-to-goodness, all-American orgasm. She then regained her composure, got dressed, and left, and we never saw her again.

It was by far the strangest thing I had seen on tour with Guns N' Roses. And I saw some strange things.

THE BUENOS AIRES MCDONALD'S

I had been on the road for two years, and I was sick of eating room service food. Actually I was sick of paying room service prices. We stayed in five-star hotels all around the world, so I was done paying $24 for a plate of pasta, and $8 for some asparagus.

So I did what any good old, red-blooded American who was yearning for a fast-food fix would do. We were in Buenos Aires, and I needed to find the nearest McDonald's restaurant.

Truth be told, we ate at McDonald's a lot in foreign countries. The food was good in the hotels, but because of the five-star thing, the portions were miniscule. We were not small guys, and we were up eighteen to twenty hours a day. We needed to eat. There were times that we could head over to the venue and eat the meals provided by the promoters, but I hardly ever got to go there, because I was with Axl 24/7, and he always ordered room service. But Axl had enough money to order two lunches, and two dinners, and even though they were small portions, the two portions were enough for him. But that would cost about $60 to $70. McDonald's? As you know, you can get about sixty cheeseburgers for that—enough to fill us up for a week.

I called the concierge downstairs of this beautiful five-star hotel in Buenos Aires, and asked the stuck-up man how close is the nearest McDonald's.

Silence. I could feel his disdain for the question.

"Are you there?" I asked.

"McDonald's, sir?"

So I condescended right back at him, "Yes, it's a restaurant that sells hamburgers."

"I'll check, sir, please hold." And just to piss me off he put me on hold for about three minutes.

He finally came back on the line and gave me the address. It was actually about three blocks from the hotel, straight down the street. I'm sure that he ate there once a week at least, but he was just too pompous to admit it.

I grabbed my wallet and headed out the door. I asked Axl if he wanted anything. He declined. I asked Robert if he wanted anything. He gave me his order, and I was off.

I very rarely left the hotel alone because of security reasons. Believe it or not, because I had long hair, people assumed I was with Guns N' Roses in some capacity.

When Guns N' Roses arrived in cities across middle America, or in cities in foreign countries, we stood out like sore thumbs. The long hair, the leather, we all just had a "look." So, when we went to the mall, or to a restaurant, or to get a haircut, or even to the local tanning salon (yes I did that once or twice on the road), people looked at us, and formed small groups. Eventually, someone from the group would come over and ask, "Are you with Guns N' Roses?" If she was a pretty girl, I answered accordingly. I know, awful, right? But I was a young, single guy then (before Natasha), so give me a break.

I looked outside the front of the hotel and there were thousands of fans standing outside to try to get a glimpse of Axl or Slash or Duff, Gilby, Dizzy Reed, or Matt, or anyone else for that matter. They were still there from the night before.

Fans in South America are awesome. They are very passionate about their favorite bands. And they will stand there for hours just to get a glimpse of their favorite bands.

Axl's room and my room overlooked the front of the hotel where these fans were parked. The night before Axl and I and a few others would open my balcony doors, and Axl would step out onto the balcony and wave to the fans. We would then join him on the balcony and marvel at the thousands of people going crazy. Then we'd head back inside.

The rest of the night we had a ball opening the door just a crack, and hearing the fans go nuts. Then we would close the door—loud sigh. Open the door, loud roar. Close the door, big sigh. This was our entertainment for the evening.

Once in a while Axl would throw something down into the crowd, and the police hated that. It would cause a gigantic free-for-all. When we saw what happened when he threw a shirt, we stopped doing that because it looked like people were getting hurt.

I readied myself for my adventure to McDonald's. I put my hair up under my baseball cap (my poor excuse for a disguise), and I walked out the front of the hotel. I walked head down, as inconspicuous as possible along the front of the hotel and around the area where the thousands of fans were standing.

Just when I thought no one had noticed that I might be with the band, two guys yelled something like, "Look over there." And they were pointing to me.

At first I didn't think much of it because they were kind of away from the crowd, but I did begin to walk a little faster. Looking back, that was the beginning of the end.

When I sped it up a little, it was a dead giveaway that I probably had something to do with the band. They started following me. Others saw them walking away from the crowd with a purpose, and they started following. Soon I could see out of the corner of my eye that this trickle effect was gaining momentum. So I started walking faster, and they started walking faster, which prompted more people to join in.

Within seconds, it became a race. I found myself running to McDonald's, and they ran after me. I thought to myself to just stop right there and explain to them that I'm not in the band, but try telling that to more than fifty people. It's impossible. And this had become way more than fifty people.

I arrived at the McDonald's, asked for a manager, and tried to explain to him that if he didn't let me go behind the counter in the next few seconds, I would be mauled by tons of people.

Thankfully, he understood and let me behind the counter just as the hundreds of fans arrived in the lobby. I headed back to the freezer so I'd be safe from the crowd.

I asked the manager of the McDonald's to explain to the crowd, in their native language, that the guy in the freezer was not in the band, and that they should all leave. Well that didn't work. No one believed him, and they figured while they were waiting they would grab a bite to eat.

This was the second to the last day of the tour. I had been through near plane crashes, drug searches, and weird strip clubs, and after all that I was going to be mauled to death, because these crazy people mistakenly thought I was in Guns N' Roses.

Great.

I immediately called for backup on my walkie-talkie.

"Security?"

"This is Earl, go."

"I'm about three blocks away, stuck in a McDonald's. I need help."

"What do you need help with?"

"Uh, hundreds of screaming fans who don't speak English think I'm in the band, and I'm hiding in the freezer in the back of a McDonald's."

Silence.

I'm sure that Earl was in a hotel room with a bunch of the guys and they were cracking up.

"Get us some Big Macs."

"Earl, I need you."

Silence.

About twenty minutes later Earl and a few other guys showed up at the local Buenos Aires McDonald's. They made their way through the crowd using their patented Guns N' Roses parting-the-crowd techniques.

They were guided to the back of the restaurant, to the freezer, where I sat, freezing my ass off.

"Hey, rock star," Earl quipped.

"Very funny."

They all had a good laugh, and they escorted me out of the McDonald's with people trying to grab and tear and pull. As we briskly walked through the crowd, I kept yelling to everyone, "I'm not in the band."

That made them even crazier.

Here's what I've learned about fans over the years: The fanatical ones will do almost anything to meet their favorite celebrity. They treat all the people that work for, or are friends with, the celebrity just as they would the celebrity, probably because they feel this is the closest they will ever get to actually meeting the celebrity.

I've had numerous fans ask me for my autograph pretty much everywhere we went. I would explain to them that they didn't want my autograph because I wasn't in the band. They'd say, "What do you do for the band?" I'd say, "I work with Axl." They'd say, "Well, that's good enough for me," and would still want my autograph, and would still try to rip my shirt off.

Crazy.

I will never understand it, but it happened all the time. For all of us on the road, I do know that we were blessed to be able to work a really cool job, in a really cool industry. But I also know that I'm just a regular guy who happened to be in the right place at the right time.

YOUR GUN FOR A HAT?

On May 22, 1993, Guns N' Roses launched the first part of their second European Tour in Tel Aviv, and it was touted, at the time, as the biggest music event ever held in Israel.

It certainly felt like it was. The whole city was buzzing about this show. Rumor had it that after the concert the local record company introduced the fourteen-year-old son of Israel's most famous male solo artist to the band . . . and the boy fainted!

This was a huge event.

We arrived a day early, and I was able to do some rare sightseeing. I rarely got out of the hotel for long, but I arranged it prior to arriving in Israel because I really wanted to go to Jerusalem. I felt that this was a once-in-a-lifetime opportunity so I asked Axl for the day off and he had no problem with it.

There were about six of us who went sightseeing in Jerusalem. The only band members with us were keyboard player Dizzy Reed and drummer Matt Sorum. Slash and Duff went with another group. I could have gone with them, but I would have spent most of the time protecting Slash from fans, as he was obviously one of the more recognized members of the band. We were the more low-key group, and except for the fact that we all had long hair, we were the more inconspicuous group.

Axl hung back at the hotel.

Normally we would take one of the limos into town, but again, we didn't want to draw extra attention, so we all squeezed into a large taxi and headed to the Old City of Jerusalem.

When we arrived we were told that our legs must be covered, and that the top of our heads must be covered as well. Most of us were wearing shorts and no hat. I was wearing jeans and my Kansas City Chiefs hat. If I didn't have my Chiefs hat, I would have had to have worn a yarmulke, and because I had jeans on I didn't have to wear a long dress-looking thing like everyone else did.

First stop, the Wailing Wall, also known as the Western Wall. This place was amazing. One tradition is to place prayer notes into the wall on tiny pieces of paper that you crumple up and stick into the cracks of the wall. I put my prayer in there, and so far everything I wrote on that note has come true.

I am very blessed.

We also visited the Church of the Holy Sepulcher, located in the Christian Quarter of the Old City. It is said to be the place where Jesus was crucified, and where Jesus was buried.

As a Christian, I was spiritually moved the entire day. We went to see a few other places, and met some very cool people.

Specifically, I met a very cool Israeli soldier.

We were just walking around the area outside the Wailing Wall, just being American tourists. The entire area is guarded by armed soldiers, and they all seemed like they were very focused on doing their jobs.

A few of us waited for Sabrina, Axl's masseuse, to come back from her area of the Wailing Wall. Women are not allowed to go to the area of the Wailing Wall that men are allowed to go and vice versa.

While we were waiting for Sabrina, an Israeli soldier walked up to our group, walked over to me, and asked, "Are you a Kansas City Chiefs fan?"

I proudly responded, "Yes I am."

He responded back, very joyfully, "So am I."

So we talked about football and how great the Chiefs were at the time.

Just a side note: I wish I could say that I put a note in the Wailing Wall asking for the Chiefs to win the Super Bowl the next year. I didn't. I did, however, say a prayer for them to win the Super Bowl while standing at the Wailing Wall.

I know, I know. All you non-football fans are thinking to yourselves, what an idiot to waste a prayer on a football team while standing in Jerusalem.

Touché.

But, all I know is this: The Kansas City Chiefs had their best season in the past thirty years in 1993 and almost made it to the Super Bowl.

Ah, the power of prayer. The way the Chiefs have been playing lately, I think it's time for me to go back to Jerusalem.

I asked the Israeli soldier if I could get a picture with him.

He said, "Of course," and we took a picture.

Then he asked, "Can I take a picture wearing your Kansas City Chiefs hat?"

I responded, "Absolutely," and I gave him my hat.

We took the next picture.

Then I asked something that when I look back on it, I think could have been the stupidest question I ever could have asked a foreign soldier.

I jokingly said, out loud, in front of all my friends, "Can I get a picture of you and I, with me holding your gun?"

My buddies were stunned. I'm sure they were all thinking, "Are you serious, dude?"

Although I knew nothing about guns, I could see that his was one badass piece of machinery, and if I had to guess, I would say it was an Uzi submachine gun.

Without a beat, he took off his gun, over his head, and handed it to me.

And we took a picture.

That's it. It was as if he just handed me a stick of gum. That's how nonchalant it was.

I didn't want to hold the gun for too long for fear another soldier, maybe one having a bad day, would see me, a long-haired dude, holding a gun, think I was a threat, and pop a cap in my ass.

So as soon as the picture was shot, I handed the gun back.

But the trust—the incredible trust this soldier had—made me feel great about being part of the human race. Gushy, I know. But I got this overwhelming feeling of brotherhood, probably because I was in a spiritual place. But it felt awesome. Yes, there are a lot of things wrong with the world we live in today, but there are also many great things about it as well.

And just so everyone out there knows, the note I wrote, and crumpled up, and put into a crack in the Wailing Wall? Well, I wrote what any good beauty pageant contestant would say. I asked for health for my family. And although my wife, Natasha, was diagnosed with Hodgkin's Lymphoma cancer in 2006, she is completely healthy now.

So, in a way, all my prayers were answered.

The next day was the show. One of the highlights of the concert was when the band and Axl, wearing a Guns N' Moses shirt, broke into a rousing rendition of "Hava Nagila."

THE PHOTO SHOOT

There was a portion of the tour in 1991 when Axl would photograph everything. He bought a new camera and really got into photography. He even had a special road case built to hold and protect his new camera. One "photo session" really stands out in my mind.

It was about two in the morning and we were leaving a show. As our limo pulled out of the backstage area Axl saw a pretty woman among the thousands of fans lining the driveway. Uncharacteristically, Axl rolled down his window and asked her if she wanted to come with us back to the hotel. In my years of touring with Guns N' Roses, that was the only time I can remember him doing that.

Of course, she agreed and jumped in the limo. At the same time the 3,727 other women wanted to follow, so Earl had to put his security hat on and handle the situation. We drove on, unscathed.

After an awkward moment of silence, Axl grabbed his camera. Without a word, he started taking pictures of the girl, and she started smiling for the camera. Innocent poses—really cute stuff.

Axl, a photography enthusiast, admiring his photographs . . . using binoculars?

Axl continued to take pictures, and she got much more comfortable, and began to really get into it. In fact, all of a sudden she started to pose as if she were doing a *Playboy* shoot.

Robert and I looked at each other and smiled as we pressed as far against our windows as possible so she had more room to get more creative with her poses.

This went on for a few minutes. Axl was just clicking away. *Click, click, click . . .*

For some reason the windows in the limo began to fog up. Maybe it's because she began to unbutton her shirt.

Axl continued to take more pictures.

Then Robert mouthed to me, "I don't think there's any film in the camera."

I just smiled.

This was 1991, and in 1991 cameras could only take thirty-six pictures at a time using film(!). No digital yet. So while Axl was clicking away, we're wondering if the woman was going to ask why Axl's camera was able to take so many pictures without reloading. We figured by now he must have clicked at least 300 pictures.

But no, she continued to lose articles of clothing, and Axl continued clicking away.

I figured she knew exactly what was going on, but just didn't care. She was in a limo with Axl Rose, and her friends weren't.

I'm sure she told that story to everyone she knew for years.

RED LION RESTAURANT & BAR, NEW YORK CITY

I'll probably never be allowed in another Red Lion Bar for the rest of my life after telling this story, but I really don't care. I don't drink anymore, so it's not an issue. Even if I did drink I would never go there again because the bouncers there in the early 1990s were obviously trained to hurt first and ask questions later.

We stayed in a hotel in New York City because for the next three nights Guns N' Roses would play at the world's most famous venue, Madison Square Garden. Since I'm originally from New York, I loved that I was going to get a chance to be part of a group playing Madison Square Garden. I would get to go backstage, and stand on the court that Walt Frazier, Willis Reed, Bill Bradley, Dave DeBusschere, and Dick Barnett stood on in 1969 when the New York Knicks won the World Championship.

I had been to the Garden numerous times in my life to watch the Knicks, The Big East Basketball Tournament (I'm a huge Syracuse fan), and to watch the New York Islanders, when they played on the road against the New York Rangers. I hated the New York Rangers, and obviously the bouncers at the Red Lion Restaurant and Bar in Greenwich Village knew that.

Kidding.

Maybe.

Anyway, because I'm from New York I felt I had an obligation to get as many tickets as possible for my family members to come see one of the GNR shows at the Garden.

My parents went to the show, and my aunts went to the show. Yes, forty-five to fifty-five-year-old men and women sat in the first few rows among the head bangers and teenagers who frequented Guns N' Roses concerts. Just to be safe, I had some of our security guys keep an eye on my family during the concert. The thought of my mom and my aunt slam dancing with a bunch of teenagers was a little too much for me to handle.

We did two shows in a row, and then we had two nights off before the third and final show. On one of the nights off, Robert and I headed into the Village to partake in a few cocktails.

The Village was a favorite place of mine from my college days. There's a gay community within the Village, and even though I'm straight I fit right in because I had an extensive background in theater. My two mentors throughout college and way into my adult life, Mark Cole and Ron Medici, were both from the theater department. Ron passed away while I was writing this book.

Robert and I took a taxi from our hotel to Bleecker Street—the heart of the Greenwich Village nightclub district. We first went to The Bitter End, a place I had frequented in college and my years after college, and then we hit a few other bars, before we ended up at one of my favorite places, The Red Lion Restaurant and Bar.

By then it was almost four in the morning, so this was going to be our last stop. We had met a couple of new lady friends, and we all were sitting at the bar having one last drink.

The entire night up until this point had been great. A couple of GNR crew guys and a few guys from the band were also on the street as well, and we had all seen each other hopping from bar to bar. It was an awesome evening. But it was time to leave. The lights were turned up in the bar, and the bouncers were asking everyone to grab their belongings and to take the last sips of their drinks. Robert got up to go to the bathroom, and I remained at the bar with our two lady friends until he returned.

People were starting to leave, and a bouncer walked over to where I was standing in the bar area and asked us all to leave.

"Bar's closed, let's go," he barked.

He had a job to do and I understood that, but I wanted to wait for Robert. The streets get packed at four in the morning because everyone spills out into the street from all the bars at the same time.

I will be the first to admit that I probably had a little too much to drink that night. But I also know that I was being singled out because of my hair and my "look."

Robert and I were on tour with Guns N' Roses, and after a while, you all start to look like each other because we're all together 24/7. It's like a married couple. After about fifteen to twenty years together you start looking like each other. It's uncanny.

Anyway, Robert and I were pretty much the only guys at the restaurant with really long hair, and we looked like rockers. We had the leather jackets, and we definitely stood out. The Red Lion Restaurant and Bar had more of a preppy crowd. Usually I would have fit in with that crowd, but not while I was touring with Guns N' Roses. We all dressed a little different.

So the bouncer focused all his attention on me.

"Let's go, we're closed," he said.

"We're just waiting for my buddy, he's in the restroom," I said.

"We're closed, come on."

"It'll just be a minute," I reiterated. "Can we just wait here?"

Getting in my face, the bouncer said, "I said, let's go."

"Dude, there are still tons of people in the bar. I'll leave when my friend gets out of the bathroom. I don't know what the big deal is."

You know how everyone has a trigger button? Well, I had just hit his. He immediately grabbed my arm, violently escorted me out of the bar, and tossed me into the street.

I had seen the "bad guy" get tossed to the pavement in movies and in cartoons, but I never quite knew this took place in real life until that moment.

I was pissed—drunk and pissed off. Not a good combination.

Our two lady friends came out to make sure I was okay. I was. But they knew I was pissed.

The bouncer who threw me out then stationed himself right outside the front entrance of the establishment.

I gave him the evil eye. He shot me the evil eye right back.

It was war, and it was on.

I started pacing back and forth in front of the restaurant, taunting him the entire time.

"You made a huge mistake, buddy."

He smirked.

"Seriously, dude, huge mistake."

Stiff as a board. He reminded me of the soldiers that guard Buckingham Palace. They never move, no matter what you say.

"I'm glad I'm not you. I have friends, dude."

I was saying all the BS that you just don't say after you've been thrown out of a bar. Textbook stuff.

I could see that I was getting to him, though, because other people heard what I was saying to him, and it looked as if he was getting embarrassed by my taunting.

Finally, Robert came out from the restroom and saw that I was pissed.

"What's going on?" he asked.

"You want to know what's going on?" I replied.

Well, I told Robert, loud enough so that the bouncer would hear my every word.

Pointing: "This guy threw me out of the bar, that's what's going on."

Robert turned to see the bouncer, a six-foot-four, probably 300-pound guy with his arms folded.

I'm sure Robert thought to himself let's get out of here, because we don't want any part of that guy.

He tried to reason with me, but it was too late. I had been ridiculed in front of my two lady friends, and the alcohol was really affecting my judgment.

I continued, "There were tons of people still left in the bar, but he wouldn't let me stay and wait for you, so he threw me out into the street. Didn't you, Mr. Bouncer Man?"

Again, no movement.

"That's right, you know I'm right, that's why you can't say anything because you know I'm right."

I was just digging deeper and deeper.

"Isn't that right?"

Again, no response.

"You're scared to answer me, aren't you."

Nothing.

Finally I said, "You're an asshole."

With that he grabbed a flashlight out of his pocket, and the first thing I thought was he's going to hit me with it.

He didn't. Instead he pointed it down the street, to his right, and turned it on and off. He then pointed the flashlight down the left side of the street and turned it on and off.

"That's right, an asshole!" I added.

Less than a second later I was attacked by the Red Lion bouncer and about five other huge bouncers from every direction.

They punched and kicked me in the head. I was getting pummeled by six or more huge guys right in the middle of the street in New York City.

My glasses went flying, and it felt like it went on for about two minutes.

Robert jumped in to try to help me, and in his rage, actually summoned the strength to get one guy off me during the attack.

He grabbed that guy, threw him up against the wall, and with his thumb, hit him in the throat and told him to lay off.

That was awesome.

They must have gotten tired from all the punching and kicking, because they finally stopped. They immediately went back to their respective bars as if nothing had happened. Not a word was said, but no words were needed. I got a good old-fashioned whuppin'.

Amazingly, I never went to the ground the entire time. I was bent over in an effort to protect myself, but I never went down. As I stood up straight I realized I wasn't in any pain. I must have been kicked and punched over fifty times, but nothing hurt. It's incredible what alcohol can do for pain.

I retrieved my glasses, which were broken. Our two lady friends were obviously in shock. I looked over to the bouncer one more time and just stared at him.

He smiled.

But this time I didn't say a word. The four of us left the area and walked over to a twenty-four-hour restaurant down the street and ate breakfast.

The next day, I guess you can say, I was in a lot of pain. I looked back on the evening and realized that what I did was completely stupid, but there are three sides to every story. In this case there was my side, the bouncer's side, and the truth.

In my mind, the truth was that I did not deserve to be singled out and thrown out of the bar. But I *did* deserve to get an ass-beating for the taunting on the street.

But not by six guys.

Earl came into my room the next day and noticed that I had been beaten up. I told him the whole story. And he said that he was going to take care of this and he left.

He was gone for the next three hours.

When he came back to the hotel, I asked him, "Earl, what did you do?"

Earl told me that he went down to the Red Lion Restaurant and Bar and spoke with the manager. It was the afternoon, so none of the night bouncers was present yet. Earl told the manager that the bouncer made a huge mistake last night, and that I was a member of the entourage of Guns N' Roses, and that we are all a close-knit team, and when you hurt one of us, you hurt all of us. And then

Earl said, "We will all be back." And he left. The manager was silent as Earl walked out the door. Remember, Earl is a very large, very strong man.

I wish I would have seen the face on the bouncer when he found out that we were with Guns N' Roses, and that we were going to come back in force.

Classic.

Of course, we never went back there—we were not those kind of guys. But I must admit that it was good to know that if something did go wrong, I had guys that would watch my back. We were family.

Bottom line: I have the utmost respect for bouncers, I really do. Especially because on our world tour security was extremely important, and I understand how vital it is to keep the peace. But this bouncer took it to another level, I'm convinced only because of the way I looked. And that just was not cool.

STRIP CLUBS

Nudity happened to be part of the Guns N' Roses tour. Whether one of us was caught naked in a hotel hallway, or women flashed their breasts for the cameras before every show, or one of us was paid to run naked through a parking lot in South America, or a fan was making love to an Indianapolis 500 car just outside the backstage dressing rooms, it seemed as though nudity was everywhere we looked.

Including, of course, strip clubs. To be honest, and this is the truth, I was never a big fan of strip clubs. It just never felt right for me, and I don't know why. Had I been to strip clubs before Guns N' Roses and Air Supply? Yes, but really only when there was a bachelor party, or a special event. I never attended a strip club just to go to a strip club.

But Guns N' Roses did. While on tour, members of the band went to strip clubs quite often. But it was almost like a hangout, like going to a bar, except this bar was filled with beautiful naked women. I was fortunate in that Axl very rarely went to strip clubs, so I didn't go as often as other members of the entourage. But when we went, we went in style.

It was VIP treatment all the way. We would walk in and be escorted to a private room, usually in the back. Somebody from the management team would sometimes hand us wads of $1 bills for the obvious reasons. I would sit there and talk to either Robert or Earl while band members got lap dances.

We went enough times in the three years on the road that it actually became boring. As I write this, it seems weird to me that seeing a naked woman could be boring, but try going to these places on a weekly basis. You get immune to it.

Then there is Japan.

Japan takes the strip club thing to a whole new level.

When I was on tour with Air Supply a few of us went out one night in Tokyo to get a drink. I think we were in the Roppongi District, and everywhere you looked there was either a bar or a strip club. We just wanted to have a drink or two at a regular bar. Besides, we were with Frank Esler-Smith, Air Supply's keyboard player, and he was gay. The last place he wanted to go was a strip club.

So we're walking down the street and each bar has a "barker" outside trying to get people to come inside. We passed a few bars when we came to a place that looked interesting, and the barker told us that we would have a good time. We told him that we just wanted to get a drink at a regular bar—no strip club. He assured us that his place was not a strip club.

We went in.

It was empty. It definitely wasn't a strip club, though, so the barker had told the truth. It actually looked more like a restaurant.

As we walked in, a Japanese fellow came out from the back room, and in broken English he put the five of us each at a separate table. We all could have easily fit at one table, but we were each now sitting at our own table.

"Okay, this is weird," someone bellowed.

Before any of us could agree, music started blasting as if a show was about to begin. The lights in the restaurant dimmed, and five Japanese girls came out from behind the black curtain and began to parade around the room.

"This is a strip club," Frank yelled.

But none of us wanted to be rude to the five girls, so we stayed to see where this was going.

The music stopped, and the five girls each slid into our individual tables. It seemed each of us had a date.

Awkward.

To make matters worse, the barker who led us into the "bar" and the host who seated us at our individual tables were both nowhere to be found. We were alone with our predetermined Japanese dates.

I heard one of the guys trying to ask his "date" a question, and she just giggled.

"Do you speak English?" he added.

Again, just a giggle.

None of these women spoke English.

We all sat there and talked to each other from our respective tables, until one of us had the nerve to make the first move to leave.

After about three minutes, Frank said, "I'm not having fun."

I started laughing. And because I was laughing, the girl I'm sitting with started to laugh as well, and I noticed that *she has no teeth*.

She couldn't have been more than twenty-two years old, and she literally had no teeth.

That did it for me. I apologized to my "date," even though I knew she had no idea what I was saying, and I got up to leave.

It didn't take long for Frank to follow me out the front door. The others immediately followed.

That was just so weird.

But even weirder than that was when I was with Guns N' Roses in Japan, and the same thing happened—a few of us decided to go out for a drink. This was about seven or eight years after the Air Supply incident. I honestly forget who was there, but it was a few members of the band, a couple of us from the entourage, and even a few guys from the crew.

We hit the same area as I had with Air Supply. It's not that this was a coincidence, everyone goes to the Roppongi District when visiting Tokyo.

So, same thing, we're walking around Roppongi, and the barkers were out in full force. Probably the same guys as before. And just like last time, a place seemed pretty cool, so we went in to check it out.

And this is what we saw . . .

There was a bar, and past the bar there was a full audience. Beyond the audience there was a small stage. And as shocking as this may seem, the audience was watching a man having sex with a woman onstage.

I was on tour with Guns N' Roses, and even though I thought I had seen everything, I had not seen this before, and if I had a vote, I wish I never saw it. It was shocking to all of us.

I don't know how long the two of them had been going at it onstage before we got there, but about two minutes after we arrived we noticed he was obviously "finished," and with that, received a standing ovation.

He got dressed, and took his seat back in the audience.

Again, shocking! I think we all just stood there with our mouths wide open.

The woman onstage left, also to applause, and the next woman came out. She looked about twenty-five years old, maybe a little older. She started to take off some of her clothing, and stood at the edge of the stage in her bra and panties.

Then she scanned the audience.

She was looking for someone from the audience to have sex with . . . onstage . . . in front of everyone.

She turned her attention to us. We were standing in the back of the room, and she called to us, "C'mon, American boy, come on."

We couldn't tell which "American boy" she was looking at, but if she was talking to me there wasn't a chance in hell that I'd go up there. My cohorts all felt the same. We each started hiding and ducking so she wouldn't choose any of us.

After a minute or two of no response from any of us, she turned her attention back to the audience and chose a Japanese man. The woman this man was sitting with seemed so happy for him. We thought it might be his wife, and maybe this was some kind of birthday present.

This was one weird, funky place, and as soon as that guy got onstage and started taking his clothes off we were out of there.

That was too much for even Guns N' Roses.

As we left the building a large tour bus pulled up right where we had just exited. The doors to the bus opened and out came about thirty to forty men and women in their late sixties, or seventies, at least. They all walked straight into the bar that we just left. Giggling.

They were going to see a "show." That was just so wrong!

AXL KILLS A MOTH

Right now you're thinking "Big deal." Boring story, right? Axl killed a moth. So what. But this is actually one of my favorite stories.

When we were fortunate enough to be off the road for more than a week, we all got to go home to see our families. I always went home with Axl, because even off the road, I still worked with him full-time. Every day, I'd drive up to his house in Malibu, do some advance work for the next leg of the tour, take care of some house stuff, handle all his personal matters, and so on.

One afternoon a moth got into the house. An uninvited, very rude moth. Obviously this moth was a huge fan of Axl's because it *would not leave* no matter how many times we asked it to. Robert was there, too, and he and I tried and tried, but the moth ignored us and kept flying around Axl's dining room chandelier.

Well, at some point, Axl had had enough. He was absolutely determined to get rid of that pesky moth. Most people at this point would get a ladder or a chair and a flyswatter and go to work.

Most people.

But not a rock star.

And especially not Axl Rose.

Axl instructed me to keep a close eye on it, and he ran upstairs. So, there I was, watching a moth and worrying about how pissed Axl would have been if I had let it out of my sight. If someone could have taped me tracking that moth from room to room, I would have won $100,000 on *America's Funniest Home Videos*, no contest.

When Axl finally came back he's wasn't carrying a flyswatter. He was carrying a gun. Not a pistol, but a long gun. A rifle maybe, or even a shotgun.

Now, I'm not a gun expert. In fact, this may be hard to believe for some, but I have never shot a gun in my life. And what might be harder to believe is that I've never even held a gun in my entire life. I've shot BB guns before, but that's it. So when I say I'm not an expert in guns, I truly mean it.

My first thought was, *Thank God I know where that moth is, otherwise Axl would probably shoot me.* But at that point it was obvious that the gun wasn't for me—it was for the rude moth.

Axl was on a mission.

Rock stars do everything bigger and better.

It wasn't enough for Axl to just shoot the moth. No, he insisted on setting up a barrier so that just in case he missed (though how you could miss anything with a shotgun at a range of less than ten feet I don't know), he would be safe behind his own personal wall. You know, in case the moth chose to attack or something.

Axl said, "Get me a chair."

I brought over a dining room chair (a really nice chair—it was Axl's house).

Axl positioned himself *under* the chair, lying on his back, using the seat of the chair as cover from the potential killer attack moth.

"Okay, dude, make him go into the corner," instructed Axl.

"Do what?" I said.

"Get the moth to come out from the chandelier, into the corner so I can shoot it. I don't want to hit the light."

Right.

As I stood on another (really nice) dining room chair, I thought, *If I do, miraculously, get the moth to go into the corner, how will it stay there so Axl can shoot it? Does Axl want me to stay close to the moth so it doesn't fly back into the light? Does Axl want me to stay there while he shoots the moth?*

I was getting paid very well at that time, but the thought of standing between Axl and a moth, with Axl holding a gun, was very stressful. But dealing with stress was a key part of the job, and I was used to doing what I was told, so I stood there.

Today I'm much older and don't have a death wish, and would never do that, but at the time I just trusted that Axl was a good shot, and I stayed right there, making sure the moth was cornered until Axl could shoot. Thankfully, I didn't know much about shotguns at the time, either.

"If you hand me a flyswatter, I think I could get him," I begged.

"Not going to happen," Axl said with a laugh.

So with the moth hovering in the corner of Axl's dining room ceiling, and me waving my hands frantically to make sure it stayed in the corner of the ceiling, Axl pulled the trigger, and . . .

Boom!

I checked my chest, my arms, and my legs to see if I'd been hit, and again, amazingly, I walked away unscathed.

The moth, of course, was obliterated. I didn't see more than a little dust come from the ceiling after the shot. But the moth was indeed gone.

After a victory yell by all of us in the room, Axl calmly got to his feet and walked off into the sunset, victorious. (Actually he walked back upstairs to his bedroom to put the gun away.)

Now, I don't know why there wasn't a gigantic hole in the wall. My best guess is that Axl just happened to have a shotgun around that he had preloaded with rock salt or something, because there were lots of little holes in the area where the moth breathed its last breath (if moths even breathe). It could have been a BB gun that shot out lots of little BBs or pellets. But I don't give a rat's ass what kind of gun it was, all I know is that the moth was defeated.

Some people talk about killing flies with sledgehammers. But that's just a metaphor. Axl Rose really did kill the dreaded Malibu moth with a gun. And for him, it was just another day in the life of a rock star.

Axl, using his dining room chair as a shield, attempting to destroy the "killer" moth.

Me, Sabrina Okamoto (Axl's masseuse), and Mike Hall (part of the GNR management team) in front of thousands of fans outside one of our hotels.

Earl (wearing Slash's top hat), Axl, and me walking through the "secret" entrance of a hotel to avoid the thousands of fans waiting outside.

Handing out Guns N' Roses photos to crazed fans in South America.
Go Chiefs.

Fans starting to assemble outside of our hotel in South America.

STARS

FREDDIE MERCURY TRIBUTE

Monday, April 20, 1992, the fifth greatest day of my life. The first four were: the day I got married, and the births of my three sons. There, I'm good with my family now for another ten years at least.

But truly, the Freddie Mercury Tribute Concert was a very special day for me. For the two of you who don't know, Freddie Mercury was lead singer of the mega-popular band Queen. In 1991, Freddie Mercury passed away from AIDS-related causes. A year later the three other members of Queen, Brian May, Roger Taylor, and John Deacon, decided to hold a concert in honor of Freddie Mercury, and to help create AIDS awareness.

The music industry responded. Many huge rock stars showed up to perform, and it was an amazing concert. Stars included Elton John, Robert Plant, David Bowie, Annie Lennox, Elizabeth Taylor, Liza Minnelli, George Michael, Lisa Stansfield, and, of course, Guns N' Roses.

Growing up, I idolized Freddie Mercury. I am a *huge* Queen fan. I bought every album, I knew every song, and I knew every word to every song. In fact, I wanted to be Freddie Mercury when I grew up. I sang to records in my bedroom, pretending I was him, performing onstage in front of millions of fans. I knew all his moves and nuances. Now I was in London at the world-famous Wembley Stadium, helping Axl Rose of Guns N' Roses get ready for the concert of the decade.

I was jazzed.

Guns N' Roses performed their Bob Dylan cover, "Knockin' On Heaven's Door," and their hit encore song, "Paradise City." Later that night Axl joined Elton John and the other members of Queen for an amazing version of "Bohemian Rhapsody." Axl also performed "We Will Rock You" with Queen, and Slash played "Tie Your Mother Down" together with Queen and Joe Elliot of Def Leppard. The show was broadcast live around the world via satellite, and it had the largest audience for a music concert in music industry history.

Because I was Axl's liaison I got to meet tons of celebrities. They would come backstage and Doug Goldstein would bring them to Axl's dressing room because they wanted to meet Axl. Doug would ask me if Axl was ready or if he was in the mood. So I got to meet everyone.

Like the time GNR did a show at Slane Castle in Ireland. Ron Wood of the Rolling Stones needed a ride and we were flying in because Slane Castle has one road in and one road out. So bands would take a helicopter there. Ron Wood probably knew he wasn't going to drive there, so while we're all standing around, I heard Ron say, "Mind if I catch a ride?" And so I shared a helicopter with a Rolling Stone.

I also met Elton John—Sir Elton John. I had met him previously at the MTV Awards when he and Axl sang "November Rain"

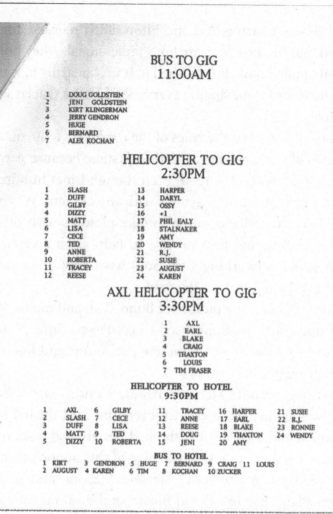

BUS TO GIG
11:00AM

1 DOUG GOLDSTEIN
2 JENI   GOLDSTEIN
3 KIRT KLINGERMAN
4 JERRY GENDRON
5 HUGE
6 BERNARD
7 ALEX KOCHAN

HELICOPTER TO GIG
2:30PM

1	SLASH	13	HARPER
2	DUFF	14	DARYL
3	GILBY	15	OSSY
4	DIZZY	16	+1
5	MATT	17	PHIL EALY
6	LISA	18	STALNAKER
7	CECE	19	AMY
8	TED	20	WENDY
9	ANNE	21	R.J.
10	ROBERTA	22	SUSIE
11	TRACEY	23	AUGUST
12	REESE	24	KAREN

AXL HELICOPTER TO GIG
3:30PM

1 AXL
2 EARL
3 BLAKE
4 CRAIG
5 THAXTON
6 LOUIS
7 TIM FRASER

HELICOPTER TO HOTEL
9:30PM

1	AXL	6	GILBY	11	TRACEY	16	HARPER	21	SUSIE
2	SLASH	7	CECE	12	ANNE	17	EARL	22	R.J.
3	DUFF	8	LISA	13	REESE	18	BLAKE	23	RONNIE
4	MATT	9	TED	14	DOUG	19	THAXTON	24	WENDY
5	DIZZY	10	ROBERTA	15	JENI	20	AMY		

BUS TO HOTEL

1	KIRT	3	GENDRON	5	HUGE	7	BERNARD	9	CRAIG	11	LOUIS
2	AUGUST	4	KAREN	6	TIM	8	KOCHAN	10	ZUCKER		

Travel itinerary for the Slane Castle gig in Ireland.

together. Both he and Axl were playing their own piano, and Elton asked me if I liked his cup.

And then I met Elton again at the Freddie Mercury Tribute. Elton had wanted to rehearse "Bohemian Rhapsody" with Axl, but Axl was going through some relationship issues with Stephanie Seymour, so just getting to the show was going to be hard for Axl. But he did the show, and it was amazing. Axl and Elton didn't rehearse for even one second, but because they are both professionals, they pulled it off. Not only pulled it off, but crushed it. It was amazing to watch— Axl Rose and Elton John singing everyone's favorite Queen song.

Incredible.

I met tons of stars, but the rules of the road were that you didn't take pictures of other celebrities and rock stars, because you were "with the band." So on the road, even though I met hundreds of celebrities, I never took any pictures with any of them. When I am speaking, I teach businesspeople to take pictures with business leaders, celebrities, and anyone else to help get a conversation started on social networking sites. So, I wish now I had pictures of me and everyone I met on the road.

Actually, I do have one picture of Bono, Axl, and me backstage at one of our concerts. Bono used to come see Guns N' Roses, and Axl and I would go see U2 a few times. Axl and Bono were huge fans of each other.

However, the Freddie Mercury Tribute Concert was different. Everyone was taking pictures with everyone, so I dusted off my 35mm camera and brought it with me. I bought about six rolls of film because I wanted to take advantage of this opportunity.

I took pictures of everyone. Me and Liz, me and Liza, me and Robert Plant, me and David Bowie, and even me and Spinal Tap. The list goes on and on. I even took a picture of Liz Taylor moments after she walked into Slash's dressing room backstage, and saw Slash in all his glory. Rumor has it that she wasn't embarrassed and didn't quite leave right away. And she wasn't looking into his eyes. Hysterical.

I was taking so many damned pictures that I kind of forgot that I was working for Guns N' Roses. Axl was about to take the stage to sing "Paradise City," and I was holding his cool UK leather jacket that he wanted to wear for the song. Usually, Earl

My only picture of me and Axl.

and I escorted Axl onto the stage, but as I heard Roger Taylor say: "Please welcome Guns N' Roses," I was still about a hundred feet from the stage.

"Oh damn!" I screamed.

I ran faster than I have ever run before to get Axl his jacket.

When I got to him I could see he was looking for my happy ass. I tossed him his jacket and he just glared at me. I smiled, and I think he was a bit perturbed. But at that moment I really didn't care because he got his jacket in time, and I got some incredible pictures.

"Paradise City" was a huge hit, and I know I'm a little biased here, but Guns N' Roses stole the show. They were incredible and the crowd was totally rocking.

After the performances we all hung backstage for a few hours, and shared war stories from the road. There were no egos that day, and everyone treated the rock stars, and guys like me, with respect, as if we were all on the same team. It was my most memorable experience ever while on the road with both Air Supply and Guns N' Roses.

But the night didn't end there.

Axl usually didn't go out after a show. But because he hadn't performed his usual two-and-a-half-hour show, he decided that he would go out on the town with some of the other stars.

We took our limo to a local bar/restaurant. It was Axl, Earl, and me, and we hung with Liz Taylor, Liza Minnelli, Elton John, and George Michael. I was pinching myself to make sure this was all really happening.

We had a few drinks and I think a few appetizers, and suddenly, out of nowhere, Axl says, "Let's go."

When Axl says, "Let's go," we go.

So Earl and I got up from the table. I grabbed my leather jacket from the back of my seat. It got caught on something, but because Earl and Axl were already halfway out of the door, I ripped my jacket from the chair and ran out the door. No kisses good-bye with Liz and Liza, no hugs for Elton or George, we were gone faster than a kid stealing from a candy store.

As usual, our limo was waiting for us in front of the restaurant. We dodged a few fans, jumped in the limo, and sped off, back to the hotel.

As I got settled in the back of the limo, I checked my coat pocket for my camera and my rolls of film. They were gone. I checked in and around the seats of the limo—no camera or film. It must have fallen out of my pocket as we left.

Since the hotel was only about five minutes away, I didn't say anything to Axl. I figured I would get him back in his room, and I would take the limo back to the bar.

And I did just that. But it took way longer than the twenty minutes I had estimated it would take.

So about an hour later I asked the driver to take me back to the bar. I ran in and I checked in and around the table where I had sat. But Elton, Liza, Liz, and George weren't there anymore, and the table was occupied by a new group of people. I asked around if anyone had seen a camera and film, but no luck. In one hour, all my memories of the fifth greatest night of my life were gone.

Thank goodness I still have pictures of the top four days of my life.

Just think, some person in London has all these great pictures of some of the biggest stars in the world, hanging out with me, a guy that nobody knows.

But here is the benefit of writing a book and social media. Hopefully, the person who found my film back on April 20, 1992, is reading this book. And hopefully, he or she developed my film and didn't throw the pictures away. Because it would be so cool, and make for a great story, if I got all those pictures back more than twenty years later.

GIANNI VERSACE & VICTORIA'S SECRET MODELS

In addition to teaching outside-the-box marketing tools to entrepreneurs all over the United States, I also talk a lot about joint ventures (partnerships), and how powerful they can be when trying to grow your business.

One of my favorite joint venture stories features two music stars from two totally different generations: David Bowie and Bing Crosby. These two music icons teamed up to perform the Christmas song "The Little Drummer Boy." At first it seemed strange that two artists from completely different genres would get together. But when the song hit the airwaves David Bowie's audience immediately knew who Bing Crosby was, and Bing Crosby's older audience immediately knew who David Bowie was. And each of their audiences became fans of the other musician, and started buying their albums. The song, and the video that accompanied the song, were both huge hits.

I continue to show the Bowie/Crosby music video at all my seminars when I talk about partnerships. If positioned correctly, joint ventures are a win-win situation for both parties.

Axl was dating Victoria's Secret model Stephanie Seymour back in 1992. So Axl, me, and usually Robert and Earl would be invited to some cool events in the fashion world. Let me clarify—Axl would be invited, and we were just there for support and security.

So because Stephanie was a supermodel, she had a connection to Gianni Versace. Gianni Versace was known as one of the top designers in the fashion industry. Very expensive, very high-end clothing. Versace was at the top of the fashion world, and Guns N' Roses were at the top of the music industry. A perfect match.

Eventually someone, probably Doug or Axl, came up with the idea of a joint venture with Guns N' Roses and Versace. At first, you'd look at that and say, "Not a chance in hell." But as you look a little closer it made total sense.

All of a sudden instead of the typical black tour T-shirt with the Guns N' Roses logo, our staff T-shirts were now made by Versace. We were all loving this. Because they were so valuable, I still own about twelve Versace tour shirts that say Guns N' Roses on the front, with either Staff, or Crew, or Security on the back with the Versace logo. My guess is that each T-shirt was probably valued between $500 to $1,000 because of the designer's name.

Besides the T-shirts, we also received boxes at each hotel on the road filled with more Versace T-shirts, Versace sunglasses, and silk Versace dress shirts. The boxes were worth thousands of dollars each. There was a frenzy every time a new box would arrive.

The relationship between Versace and Guns N' Roses, specifically Axl, really took off. In June of 1992, while in Italy, Axl, Earl, and I went to Milan and visited the showrooms of Versace and Armani. They spared no expense and rolled out the red carpet for us.

We stayed for a while at Gianni Versace's main store in Milan, and hung with Paul Beck, a former American model who, at the time, was married to Gianni Versace's sister, Donatella. Paul was awesome. Really great guy, and very down to earth. Axl bought a few things, and Earl and I just tried on clothes just because that's what you do at Gianni Versace's store in Milan. But we had no intention of buying anything because, if I recall, the minimum price to buy any article of clothing there was about $200. And I think that was for a plain T-shirt.

The Versace line was always known for its vibrant colors. So Paul Beck grabbed a pink Versace jacket off the rack and handed it to me, and he told me to try it on.

I did.

I understand that pink is the new black today, but back in 1992 pink was not worn by many straight men.

But I tried it on, I looked in the mirror, and it looked awesome. I fell in love with this jacket immediately. So much that I felt like buying it.

Unfortunately, they don't do price tags at Versace's store in Milan, so I had to ask how much the jacket was. I knew I wasn't going to like the price, and therefore wasn't going to buy it. But I did ask.

Paul informed me that the jacket was $1,500.

I almost fell down. However, I tried to play it cool, and not show the horror I felt inside. I calmly put the jacket back on the rack and said, "Not bad, but let me look around a little more."

Not bad? Why the hell did I say that? What I wanted to say was, "Fifteen-hundred dollars? Are you flipping serious?"

But I didn't dare say that. Anyway, I wasn't going to spend $1,500 on a pink jacket even though it did look cool.

But then Axl turned to Paul and told him to bring the pink jacket. Paul did, and Axl laid it on top of his clothes.

"We'll take this, too," Axl said to the cashier.

"Seriously?" I asked.

"It looked good," Axl added.

"Thanks, dude." We always called each other dude.

That was so cool. Axl bought me a $1,500 pink Versace jacket.

I loved it so much that I wore it at my wedding rehearsal dinner a year later, and I still have the jacket. Doesn't fit anymore, but I kept it all these years.

That night, Axl, Earl, and I went to dinner with Paul, Donatella Versace, Naomi Campbell, and Stephanie Seymour. Christy Turlington was supposed to come but had to cancel at the last minute.

Pretty awesome lineup.

After dinner we went to Paul and Donatella's home in Milan and stayed the night. This was probably the most beautiful home I have ever seen in my life.

The next day Axl, Earl, and I attended a Versace fashion show. Now that was cool. We had front-row seats, and Gianni Versace was presenting his new line of designs. I had never been to a fashion show before, and not only was I at one with Axl, but the three of us were treated like kings.

Because we had all-access passes, we were allowed to go backstage during the show to see things behind the scenes. We flashed our passes to a large man guarding the backstage door, and we entered what I can only describe as the forbidden zone. Straight men should not be allowed here because it is a candy factory for adult men.

It was frantic. I thought it was crazy at a Guns N' Roses concert, but this was way crazier. In fact, the fashion show world had something that the rock world had a taste of, but the fashion world took it to a new level.

Naked women. There were naked models everywhere. Naked, half-naked, partially naked. All types of nakedness.

Earl and I looked at each other and all we could do was smile.

Models got out of their outfits, fixed their makeup, and put new outfits on in seconds. All out in the open. Nude models passed us on their way to get their next outfit, and say hi as they passed.

Can you understand how hard it was to look these women in the eyes and try to have a conversation while they stood there naked? Well, let me fill you in. It's impossible. How do you not look down?

We hung out for a while backstage with Gianni Versace, and we thanked him for everything. He introduced us to everyone, both clothed and not clothed. Gianni Versace was a great man, a talented designer, and a very gracious host. It was a very sad day when he was killed in front of his home in Miami only a few years later.

There were many perks when traveling with Guns N' Roses. Many perks. But I would rate my experience in Milan as one of my favorites.

SHANNON HOON

More nudity . . .

Shannon Hoon was Axl's childhood friend from Indiana, and he was lead singer of the band Blind Melon. I got to know Shannon a little when he visited Axl on the road. Shannon had sung backing vocals for "Don't Cry" from *Use Your Illusion I* and also appeared in the "Don't Cry" video. Whenever Shannon was in town during a Guns N' Roses concert, Axl brought him on stage to sing "Don't Cry."

In June 1993, Blind Melon and The Quireboys opened for Guns N' Roses at St. Jakob Stadium in Basel, Switzerland. Shannon decided to stick around after his set to watch Guns N' Roses play that night.

Halfway through the Guns N' Roses set, Shannon walked to where I stood on the side of the stage, enjoying the show with a few other members of the entourage. He was wearing a Viking helmet and carrying a large pizza box. If you knew Shannon, this wasn't out of character, so we thought nothing of it.

However, without warning or notice, Shannon put the pizza box on a road case and began to take off his clothing. All of his clothing.

He was now completely naked.

"Shannon?" I said, trying to question what he was about to do.

He just smiled at all of us, calmly grabbed the box of pizza, and headed out onto the stage in front of 80,000 screaming fans.

It was awesome. We knew he would be arrested, but it was still awesome. In fact, it was so Shannon Hoon.

He walked directly over to Axl, who was is in the middle of a song during the acoustic part of the show, and shook Axl's hand.

The band continued to play, even though they were all laughing hysterically.

Without a beat, Shannon walked over to the congas and joined in on the song (without the Domino's Pizza shirt).

He played the rest of the song completely naked.

When the song finished, the crowd went nuts. Axl just shook his head, probably thinking to himself that the press would have a field day with this one. Shannon got up, waved to the crowd, took a well-deserved bow, and calmly walked off the stage with both wrists placed in front of him, straight into the handcuffs of two awaiting police officers.

It was the easiest arrest I had ever witnessed. We all figured Shannon had done this before.

One of the police officers grabbed Shannon's clothes, and they took him straight into their police car, to the local station, without incident. I assume he was booked on either poor playing of the congas, or indecent exposure, one of the two. I also assume he got out of jail either that night or the next day, but I never found out because we were on to the next city, and we had a lot of work to do.

We all knew that Shannon was going to be okay.

How wrong we were.

Two years later, Shannon was found dead on his tour bus from a heart attack due to a drug overdose, just three months after his baby girl was born. He was only twenty-eight.

Very sad.

U2

And even more nudity . . .

One of my favorite bands of all time is U2. I've loved them since college and used to "cruise the Boulevard" with "Sunday, Bloody Sunday" blasting out of my dad's Cortina. A Cortina is a car just in case you didn't know.

One of Axl's favorite bands at the time was also U2.

While touring Europe, Guns N' Roses shared the *MGM Grand* airplane with Bruce Springsteen and U2. There must be some sort of system that booking agents follow for Europe because it seemed that we were all following each other on our respective tours. Guns N' Roses would do a show, and a few days later, U2 would come into town and do a show at the same place we just left. Same thing with Bruce Springsteen.

This type of scheduling allowed us to see the other bands perform live, specifically U2.

In May 1992, Guns N' Roses performed in Vienna, Austria, at a venue next to the famous Danube River to a sold-out crowd of 70,000 people. After the show Bono came backstage, and I hooked him up with Axl. For the next hour, Bono and Axl got into a discussion about *something*. It looked fun, animated, and it was great to watch. Every once in a while I listened in. But after a minute or two, I would walk away not knowing what the hell they were talking about.

Later that night—let me clarify, early the next morning—Bono invited us to a birthday party for U2's accountant, Ossy Kilkenny, at a Viennese restaurant. When I heard that, I prayed that Axl wanted to go because I so wanted to go to a private party with Bono and the rest of U2.

Axl agreed to go. Awesome.

When Axl, Earl, and I pulled up in our limo, the outside of this Viennese restaurant looked more like the local pub. That was a plus. I loved going to small European pubs. The people are down to earth, and there are no egos at all.

When we entered, it was definitely a small pub, with large wooden picnic tables and long wooden benches for sitting. It was a perfect setting for a bunch of Irish guys who wanted to drink beer and have fun.

As we walked through the front door, we noticed that this party had been going on for a few hours, while Guns N' Roses was onstage a few miles away.

We also noticed that it was time to bring out the birthday cake because Bono was making a speech about Ossy, more like a roasting, and he said something about the cake.

The lights dimmed.

And with that, out from the kitchen, holding over his head a large sheet cake with tons of lit candles, came the wild and crazy bass player of U2, Adam Clayton.

And he was naked.

He walked through the crowd of about a hundred people, with his penis out there for the world to see, and proudly presented Ossy with his cake.

Axl, Earl, and I looked at each other and I know we all thought, *Why couldn't we have come just a few minutes later?*

After the shock of seeing Adam naked, we settled in, had some food, drank some beer, and hung with U2 in a small pub somewhere in the outskirts Vienna.

If only the neighbors down the block knew who was in the modest little pub down the street.

The next night U2 had a show in Vienna at the same venue GNR played the night before, and we all went to see it. I think the entire band was there, and lots of members of the entourage. Halfway through the show Axl joined Bono and The Edge onstage and they played an acoustic version of "Knockin' on Heaven's Door." Guns N' Roses covered that song on *Use Your Illusion II*, and they sang it every night at their show. They performed the song on a small circular stage at the end of a walkway about fifty yards from the main stage in the middle of the crowd.

The audience went nuts.

It was the epitome of rock n' roll—an impromptu collaboration in front of 70,000 fans with no rehearsal.

About a month later, we finished the European leg of the tour. We had been in Europe for more than forty-five days, and we all really wanted to head back home for a small, much-needed break.

On the way to Los Angeles, Axl wanted to see U2 one more time, so we rented a Learjet, and Axl, Earl, and I headed to Verona, Italy. Verona is a smaller city and the hotel we stayed in seemed to be away from it all, so this was a great opportunity to hang with U2 without the huge crowds and all the distractions.

And that's what we did. We hung by the pool with the band and their entourage, I played pool (billiards) for a few hours with The Edge, and Adam kept his clothes on the entire time.

We went to the U2 show that night, again experiencing the full red-carpet treatment, and just sat on the side of the stage, enjoying the show.

Sometimes when you meet a celebrity you are disappointed because you have this idea of what they're supposed to be and how they're supposed to act, and they don't meet those expectations. It happened to me numerous times on the road with Guns N' Roses, because part of my job was to meet and interact with tons of celebrities who wanted to meet Axl Rose. To be honest, some were complete assholes.

But U2 was class all the way. From the band members to the crew, they treated us like family whenever we were around. That was rare, and very much appreciated.

KURT, COURTNEY, FRANCES BEAN, & ANDREW DICE CLAY

There are so many versions of the Axl Rose / Kurt Cobain story and since I was there, I will share exactly what happened on September 9, 1992, at the MTV Video Music Awards at UCLA's Pauley Pavilion in Los Angeles.

Guns N' Roses was going to be presented with the Video Vanguard Award, also known as the Lifetime Achievement Award, presented to musicians who have made a profound effect on the MTV culture. They were also going to play "November Rain" with Elton John. Axl was very excited to play with Elton John, and I was very excited to meet him.

Nirvana was scheduled to play their song "Lithium." I heard that MTV wouldn't allow Nirvana to play their song "Rape Me" for obvious reasons, but Kurt played a few bars live before they played "Lithium." A bit of a slap in the face, but pretty harmless.

Outside Pauley Pavilion were a plethora of trailers, used as dressing rooms for all the bands and stars appearing at the awards show that night.

Nirvana had a trailer, and in the next row over, Guns N' Roses had a trailer.

At this point in their careers it had been documented that Axl and Kurt did not get along. Kurt said things about Axl. Axl said things about Kurt. They definitely had a past, so it was weird that the promoters of the event put the two bands' trailers that close to each other.

Stephanie Seymour and Axl wanted to take a walk around the backstage area to just relax, and maybe visit some industry friends. As always, Earl and I tagged along.

The four of us arrived at the hospitality tent, and as we walked by we saw Kurt Cobain and Courtney Love, sitting at a table, eating, with their new baby, Frances Bean.

This is where the story starts to vary. And this is where the media and/or secondhand accounts have blown this "meeting of the minds" way out of proportion.

No matter what was said, it never really escalated into anything.

As we walked by, Courtney sarcastically asked Axl, "Do you want to be godfather to our daughter?"

Stephanie said something about being a model. Courtney said something about being a brain surgeon. Silly fun.

Axl then told Courtney to shut up . . . blah, blah, blah . . .

And that was it. It was quick; it was said in passing; it was really nothing. Yet, there are so many different accounts on what was said, and how it was said, that it makes us all laugh, because it was nothing.

It was so nothing that Earl and I did nothing, except smile. And the four of us went on our merry way.

That's it. When I saw it in the papers the next day I was amazed that this was a "story."

Now, what was really interesting was what happened next. As we continued our leisurely walk backstage we saw comedian Andrew Dice Clay talking to a man dressed in a suit. As we got closer we heard Dice Clay begging this man (we come to find out), an MTV executive, to let him appear on the awards show that night.

It wasn't going well for Mr. Dice Clay.

In 1989, Andrew Dice Clay was banned from MTV because he veered way off a prepared script when he was supposed to introduce Cher. And when he veered off, apparently he said some pretty crude things on live television. MTV did not like that.

Well this trying-to-mend-the-past thing was not working. Not even close. I actually felt bad for Dice Clay—it was really sad. No matter what Dice Clay said to this guy, he kept getting turned down. It was really weird watching a guy who was over-the-top onstage be very vulnerable when confronted with a real-life situation.

We finally got back to the GNR trailer, and we could immediately see that something was brewing. A potential fistfight between Guns N' Roses and Nirvana. Earl and I looked at each other and I said, "Damn, news travels fast." I assumed that this potential fight was because of the "discussion" Axl and Kurt had minutes prior in the hospitality tent. But it wasn't. This was a whole new fight.

Since I wasn't there I won't pretend I know exactly what happened, but when we got back Duff was pissed and he kept trying to get all of us to go over to Nirvana's trailer to kick some ass. He even tried to get the Nirvana guys to come out of their trailer by yelling obscenities at the closed trailer.

Luckily Doug stepped in, and the rest of our entourage calmed the band members down, so nothing happened.

Great day of music. No fights. Made for a very enjoyable day.

STEVEN TYLER

On June 5, 1992, Guns N' Roses got together at a rehearsal and sound check with Lenny Kravitz, Jeff Beck, and Steven Tyler and Joe Perry from Aerosmith, for a Live Pay-Per-View show the next day in Paris.

Lenny Kravitz, who would play his hit "Always on the Run" (Slash played guitar on the single), and Jeff Beck were scheduled to join Guns N' Roses for a couple of songs during the set, followed by an incredible encore with Steven Tyler and Joe Perry, playing their cover version of the Yardbirds song "Train Kept A-Rollin'."

The day of the huge show got off to a rocky start when Jeff Beck woke up with a nasty pain in his right ear, a recurrence of tinnitus. Both Slash and Jeff discussed the options, and they decided that Jeff shouldn't risk his hearing for one show. Slash said that he was honored just rehearsing and hanging with the famed guitarist.

But as they say, the show must go on, and that's exactly what happened. Guns N' Roses and the guest artists all headed over to the Vincennes Hippodrome, where 58,000 fans awaited their arrival onstage.

The show featured Axl (wearing a shirt that said, "I'm a Lesbian") dedicating the song "Double Talkin' Jive" to movie actor Warren Beatty.

The show ended, and as usual, the band returned for encores, this time joined by Steven Tyler and Joe Perry. They played the classic Aerosmith hit "Mama Kin" and "Train Kept A-Rollin'," before Guns N' Roses closed the two-and-a-half-hour show themselves with "Don't Cry" and "Paradise City."

But before all this happened, before this amazing show took place, I had the pleasure of meeting Steven Tyler the day before in a very unique situation.

As mentioned before, I ran Axl's teleprompter when I first started with the band, and Robert took over those duties from me. We had the words to every song in the Guns N' Roses repertoire, but when the band sang a song by another band, we had to enter the words into the computer so they would appear on the monitors and Axl could sing the song.

These days, that's easy. You Google the name of the song, and voila, you have the words. A simple copy and paste, and you're done.

Not so in the dark ages of the early 1990s.

So Axl asked me to, "Go to Steven's room and get the words to 'Train Kept A-Rollin'."

"Steven?" I said.

"Steven Tyler?" he said, obviously.

Okay, that was a stupid question. Steven Tyler was staying in the hotel so I guess I should have put two and two together.

So I grabbed a pen and a pad of paper and headed down to Steven Tyler's room, thinking to myself as I get into the elevator that this will probably be the coolest thing I will do on tour with Guns N' Roses. In my mind this was going to be great. Awesome, in fact. But what happened was way better than I could have ever imagined.

The elevator arrived on Steven's floor, and I walked down the hallway to his room. I started to get nervous because I thought he might be insulted that I didn't know the words to a famous song they covered.

Oh, crap. This was going to be weird, uncomfortable. What was I going to say?

I've always been a believer in winging it, so I knocked on his door, and I figured I'll just say whatever comes to mind and pray that I don't make an ass of myself.

Steven Tyler, the lead singer of Aerosmith, opened the door, dressed in only a towel.

"Hey, Steven, my name is Craig and I work with Axl, and we need the words to 'Train Kept A-Rollin' for tonight's show, so just in case you and Axl are having too much fun onstage, I'll have them for both of you on our stage monitors."

Immediately, I thought to myself, *Did I just imply that Steven Tyler might, himself, forget the words to his song?*

But without missing a beat Steven says, "Sure, dude, come on in."

I walked in. No one else was in the room, just Steven, his towel, and me.

Awkward.

Getting right to the job at hand, Steven said, "You ready?"

"Uh, yes. How do you want to do this? Do you have the words somewhere? I can just make a copy."

"I'll sing it to you. You ready?"

I thought I said I was ready, but I must have just said nothing, because he repeated himself.

"You ready?"

"I'm ready."

Steven started singing "Train Kept A-Rollin'" a cappella, and it sounded great.

I was such an Aerosmith fan, and for the first time on tour I actually felt like one of the Guns N' Roses fans that I encountered every day. I was so entranced by listening to his amazing voice, that I forgot to continue writing after about the third word of the song.

He finished the first verse, and he asked, "Did you get all that?"

I looked down at the three words on my pad of paper and told him, "I'm a slow writer. I got 'Train Kept A' . . . and then I lost you."

Now I'm thinking he's going to quickly get impatient real soon, but instead he said, "Okay, here it is again."

And he started singing the song again from the beginning.

This time I frantically wrote down the words as best I could, all the time thinking: *I'm getting a free concert, in a five-star hotel room, in Paris, from the lead singer of Aerosmith.* And it all hit me at once: *This is awesome!* And: *How in the hell did I get here? How did all this happen?*

And while I wrote the words down, I looked back on the day, nine years before, when Robert Street asked me if I wanted to go on tour with Air Supply. The day that changed my life forever, and I thanked God at that moment for all the blessings in my life.

All in all, Steven Tyler sang the words to "Train Kept A-Rollin'" about eight times until I had the entire song on paper.

Steven Tyler is a true rock star. But more than that, Steven Tyler is a great person, one of the best, if not the best, people I met on the road while touring with Air Supply and Guns N' Roses.

And this is why I believe that he remains successful to this day—twenty-two years later. Great things happen to great people.

Steven, thank you for the memory.

UFO NICK

Most of the celebrities I met on tour were really nice and very respectful. Most of them really wanted to meet Axl Rose, and I had the pleasure of being the guy they had to see first to see if Axl wanted to meet them. So, most of the celebrities were really nice to me, probably because they felt they needed to suck up to me to meet Axl. Unless he was sick, Axl agreed to meet pretty much every celebrity that came backstage.

But this is a different kind of star story.

We were in Las Vegas, and Earl, Blake, Axl, and I were staying in the MGM Grand bungalows behind the MGM Grand Hotel on the Strip. We each had our own bungalow—first class all the way. And even though we had these great rooms, we were bored again.

We were tired from traveling, and we had no desire to gamble because Axl would just be prodded there anyway, so we were stuck, as usual, in our hotel bungalows.

Then, out of nowhere, Axl said, "Let's get UFO Nick."

We looked at each other and shrugged our shoulders. We had no idea who UFO Nick was.

"UFO Nick?" I asked.

Axl had learned that there was some guy in Las Vegas that was apparently abducted by aliens and that he still has a direct link to them.

We met all kinds of people on the road, and we heard all kinds of weird stories, but this UFO guy intrigued Axl so much that he wanted me to get him.

This was typical Axl. All I had to go on was a name. I get no other information—no telephone number, no address, no hint of who he is or where he might be. Just "UFO Nick" in Las Vegas.

Just like in Czechoslovakia: "Craig, find me an English-speaking ear, nose, and throat doctor in thirty minutes."

"Okay."

And I did.

I remember Axl asking Robert, the day before our show in Istanbul, Turkey, that he wanted Classic Cokes in his dressing room the next night. This was when Coca-Cola was trying out New Coke. However, Axl loved Classic Coke, but everyone was supplying New Cokes backstage.

So Axl told Robert to get him a six pack of Classic Coke for the show the next night. Well, no one in the entire city of Istanbul had Classic Coke, so we had to fly out some Classic Coke from the United States by the next day. We flew in cans of Coke all over the world.

And that's what we did, every day.

We would do the research, and we would be very resourceful, and we would use money and our connections in each city to get things done, fast.

Well, somehow I found a number for a guy named Nick who was known in the area as UFO Nick and dialed it, and sure enough a guy named UFO Nick answered the phone, and yes, he was the one abducted by aliens.

Amazing.

I told him that Axl Rose wanted to hear his story, and he immediately said he was a fan and that he would be there that night.

Anything you want you can get, especially if you're working for Axl Rose.

So UFO Nick arrives that evening, just as it's getting dark. UFO Nick was a regular-looking guy that seemed very nice right away.

He was very excited to meet Axl.

The bungalows at the MGM are kind of in a U shape, creating a middle courtyard grassy area. That's where we all congregated to watch UFO Nick perform his "magic."

It was a beautiful night, and tons of bright stars filled the sky.

Or so we thought.

Nick started telling the story of how he was abducted by aliens, and that because he lived among them for a while, he had a direct link to them. He added that they follow his every move, and that they continually watch him on monitors on their spaceships because they love to study humans. He added that their spaceships are all hovering over earth at all times, "just in case."

We never asked, "Just in case what?" Probably because we didn't really want to know the answer.

So, we're all listening to this ridiculous story, but we're all being respectful because he seemed like a nice guy, and he was really good at telling a story. We're all nodding, as if we were interested in what he's saying, and we're all looking as if we're hanging on his every word. Even Axl is really "faking" his interest.

UFO Nick finished by telling us how he was probed and that he has a chip installed somewhere in his body—the typical alien stuff.

And with that, UFO Nick asked, "Are you ready?"

We all nodded in agreement, figuring the faster we agreed, the faster we could get back to our bungalows.

UFO Nick told us to look up in the sky and to look at all the "stars" in the sky.

"Yes, beautiful stars out tonight, Nick," I quipped.

"Well, Craig, not all of the bright lights you see in the sky are stars." *What are they, UFO Nick?* I thought to myself. "Some of those bright sparkles in the sky aren't stars at all, but in fact, they are alien spaceships."

We all just smiled, continuing to play along.

UFO Nick added, "Now, I'm going to have one of the spaceships move. Watch closely."

UFO Nick pointed up to the sky, and picked out one star and said, "You see that 'star' just to the right of that really bright star?"

"Yes," we all said in unison.

"Watch this."

While still pointing to the "star" he moved his index finger to the left, and this is going to sound crazy, but the "star" began to move, following the path of his index finger.

"Do you see the red trail?" he asked.

And sure enough, we saw a little red tail trailing the "star" while it moved. We all looked at each other in disbelief.

UFO Nick smiled.

"Pretty cool, huh?"

None of us knew what to say. We were stunned.

As God as my witness, this "star" moved. And we looked at each other like what the hell was that?

We were all thinking that this was some elaborate Las Vegas light show.

We continued to watch him move "star" after "star." Axl was eating this up. How could he not, we were now believers as well, as crazy as that sounds.

And then UFO Nick added this little nugget, "Now that you're with me, you're now on their monitors as well, and you can do this for your friends, because they are now tracking you guys as well."

What? I thought to myself. "I'm being tracked?" I said.

"Yup," Nick said enthusiastically.

As if this was a positive.

I thought to myself that I didn't want to be tracked by spaceships, and then I came to my senses and realized that this was ridiculous. But then I looked up to the sky and he's moving these damn "spaceships" everywhere.

This went on for a little while, and after he was done, UFO Nick rode off into the sunset, and we never saw him again.

We all talked to each other about what we had just witnessed, and we agreed not to mention this to anyone else in the band or the entourage until we figured out exactly what had just happened.

A few months later, we were in Santiago, Chile, hanging by the pool one night. On one side of me was Axl, and on the other side of me, in a lounge chair of his own, was Carlos Santana.

We were talking about the music business dating back to when Santana got in it, and out of nowhere Axl said, "Carlos, let me show you something interesting." And yes, you guessed it, Axl started pointing at the sky. And you can guess the rest.

I'm here to tell you that Axl pointed to the sky and started moving stars with little red trails shooting out.

I remember Carlos Santana looking up at the sky, and just saying, "Hmmm."

That's it. He seemed very interested, but just said, "Hmmm."

It gets worse. Earlier I shared about how Natasha and I met because James Hetfield of Metallica got burned badly at a show in Montreal, and because of that Natasha and I eventually got married.

On my second date with Natasha, I did the "star" thing for her. And sure enough, the star I pointed at started to move.

Within minutes, everyone in the restaurant was looking at me as if I were nuts. And Natasha immediately thought I was crazy as well, and she was tempted to climb out the bathroom window to get away from me.

Luckily for me, she came back.

But this happened time after time. Every time I showed someone the "stars," they moved.

Over the years I have come up with a theory on how this works, because I refuse to believe, in my now completely sober mind, that there are spaceships tracking human beings at all times. Bottom line: I think it's an optical illusion.

When you stare at a specific star (light) for a period of time, a little red edge appears. And if you move your index finger over to the left or to the right, our brains, because the sky is so vast, think the star is actually moving. But it's really not. It just looks like it does for a quick second or two.

Me and Slash at Axl's Halloween party at his home in Malibu. I had knee surgery that morning, but there was no way I was going to miss that party. I think I dressed as an old man because I was in a wheelchair and on crutches.

And although this is what I believe now, I have a little piece in me that still might believe that UFO Nick might have actually been abducted, because his "stars" moved way more than our "stars" did.

I haven't seen or heard from UFO Nick since that day in Las Vegas, but if you're ever in Vegas, look him up. He wasn't really that hard for me to find. But if you do have trouble finding him, just ask any alien where he is, because remember, they're tracking him every day.

Axl (corn) and me at one of his "famous" Halloween parties at his home in Malibu, CA.

Slash and Natasha at Axl's Halloween party.

CRAIG,

SEND PHOTOS TO ROBERT
HAVE DUFF'S CD AN NEW GN'R TO
PAUL HUGE, LANK + BAND - 4 OF
EACH - SEND SET TO PAUL + OTHER 3
SETS LEAVE W/LANK.
PICKUP 3 DEMO TAPES FROM
LANK, 2 FOR ME, 1 FOR JIM
MITCHELL

JIMS ADDRESS IS ON PHONE
LIST, SEND TO DIANE IF DURING
WORKING HOURS -

PAULS ADDRESS IS ON BACK OF
PHONE LIST.

THANKS.
- AXL -

Dave Gahan

PLEASE FIND OUT IF DEPECHE MODE
IS STILL PLAYING OR IN SAN DIEGO-
SEND CHAMPAGNE AND WISH DAVE LUCK
+ APPOLOGISE I COULDN'T MAKE IT -
IF HE'S STILL WITH TERESA INCLUDE HER
NAME ON CARD. PUT··· LOVE. AXL·

A typical note Axl would leave me of things that needed to be done. I wrote Dave Gahan on the piece of paper so I would remember who I was sending the champange to.

Slash and me at a restaurant in New York City. After a few drinks...

QUICK STORIES, STATS, & FACTS

7

- No drugs were allowed on the Guns N' Roses Use Your Illusion tour. One guy in our entourage smoked a joint one night and he was fired the next day. Of course there was plenty of alcohol to make up for it.
- As I've stated, while on tour I smoked three packs of cigarettes a day, while dipping Skoal at the same time. Dipping is putting chewing tobacco in your bottom lip. Lots of guys on the road dipped because it kept us awake—most of the time we were up for twenty hours a day.

  Five years after I quit I went to Robert Finkelstein's bachelor party and tried a little dip again. I just took a tiny bit and put it in my bottom lip. Within thirty seconds I turned green and got violently ill. That's how bad that crap is for you.

I quit smoking on October 20, 1992. This was an amazing feat considering that everyone else on the road continued to smoke. I started smoking a little again after the tour ended, then quit for good in 1994.

- Axl used a filter when he smoked his cigarettes.
- Ninety-nine percent of the time all members of Guns N' Roses and the entourage would all stay on the same hotel floor or on two consecutive floors. Axl would usually get the Presidential Suite, Slash and Duff would get suites, and the rest of the band members, and the manager, Doug Goldstein, would all get suites as well if they were available.
- My room was on one side of Axl's room and Earl's was on the other side. Robert was across the hall and Steve, Sabrina, Amy, and Stuart were very close by. Each band member also had their security person next to them as well.
- I did not get a tattoo. I'm pretty sure I was one of the only ones on the road that did not have a tattoo. And that was really hard, considering we had a tattoo artist tour with us. And he usually was only a few rooms away from my room in every hotel.
- Axl saved a bottle of Dom Pérignon after every show and we would write the date of the show and the city name on every bottle. We then shipped the bottles to his house in Malibu, California, where he put them on display for a while. He must have collected more than 200 bottles.
- That's me at the end of the *Making of Estranged* video. I'm talking into the camera saying that Guns N' Roses was all my idea. Axl thought it was really funny, so he added it in the video. Because of this video, the number-one question on a very popular Guns N' Roses chat room was, "Who the hell is Craig Duswalt?" I also appeared in the videos *Estranged* and *The Garden*.

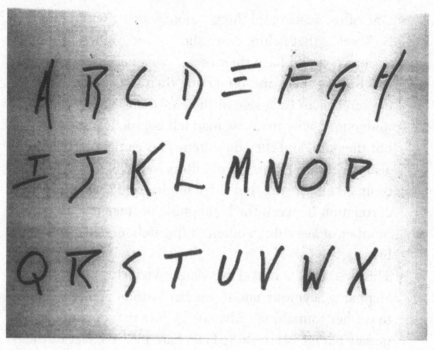

Axl Rose wrote these letters to be used for the "Estranged" video.

- Axl and Slash, especially, are two of the most disciplined people I know. Before pretty much every show Axl would get a massage from Sabrina, then get adjusted by Steve, then take a shower where he would warm up his voice for about forty-five minutes with vocal exercises, then have Steve tape his ankles, and finally go onstage. After the show he would shower, and while in the shower he would again warm down his voice for another thirty minutes. Slash was the same way. He would play scales on his guitar every day, whether there was a show or not. We can accuse Guns N' Roses of partying too much, which they did at times, but they were also very dedicated to their craft, and that is why they were so successful.

- One of the really cool things about touring with Guns N' Roses is that before every show some women in the audience would flash their breasts just because some guy was filming them and projecting their image onto the big screens on each side of the enormous stage. I never understood why many women felt compelled to do this, but they did, and they did often. This camera feed would also appear on television monitors in the band's dressing rooms. I'm not sure, but there might have been a direct correlation between the band going onstage late and the number of beautiful women in the audience showing their breasts.

- This is so rock star: Axl was dating Victoria's Secret model Stephanie Seymour, and it was her birthday, and he wanted to get her something really cool. Being the romantic he is, he saw a huge black stuffed elephant in Paris. Her birthday was the next day, and he wanted it there for her. So he had Robert book the stuffed elephant on the Concorde on a flight from Paris to New York. There's FedEx, and there's UPS, but if you're a rock star and you want to get your girlfriend a gift the next day, there is also the Concorde. By the way, this elephant is in the Guns N' Roses video for their song "Estranged." It's in the dream sequence scene where the kids are playing on the swing set in white outfits.

- We played softball with local radio stations for various charities across the United States. Gilby Clarke was the best ballplayer from the band, but most of the talent came from us—the entourage. Slash and Duff would usually play as well, and the stands would be filled with thousands of Guns N' Roses fans. When I got up to bat it felt like I was in the major leagues. Thousands of people cheering for you to get a hit. Quite the rush.

- One night, I forget where, Guns N' Roses forgot to play their biggest hit, "Welcome to the Jungle." Axl came offstage and nonchalantly said, "Damn, I think we forgot to play 'Welcome to the Jungle.'" The band members simply replied, "Hmmm." And that was it. The only time that ever happened.

- Axl loved to collect crucifixes from all over the world. He had a huge crucifix hanging in his living room.

- Axl had a pet baby wallaby on a small portion of the tour. He named him Freddie, after the late lead singer of Queen. Axl built a sling, to mimic the baby wallaby mother's pouch and carried his pet wherever he went. He also fed Freddie with a little baby's bottle. It was quite awesome to watch— Axl Rose, acting like a dad.

- Axl and I went to a few Kansas City Chiefs vs. Los Angeles Raiders football games. He's a Raiders fan. I'm smarter . . . I'm a Chiefs fan. It's actually very difficult to go to games with Axl. I love actually watching the game, but when I went with Axl, my main focus was keeping as many fans away from him as possible. But as usual, once one fan realized Axl was there, word spread quickly, and it became quite the frenzy.

- Axl must have had an affinity for kangaroos and wallabies. On the next page you'll see a picture of Axl and his new friends, Mr. and Mrs. Kangaroo. We went to an animal reserve in Sydney, Australia, and we found out fast that all kangaroos do all day long is have sex. I wanted to take regular pictures of kangaroos, but all I have is pictures of kangaroos having sex, because that's all they do. There must have been twenty kangaroos having sex at the same time. It was like I was watching a backstage orgy, not that I ever saw anything like that while touring with Guns N' Roses.

Axl and a couple of kangaroos having a grand old time in Australia.

Axl with his "pouch" to hold his pet wallaby, Freddie.

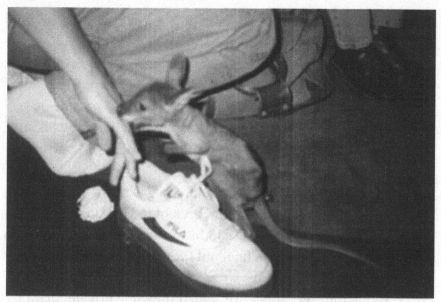

Freddie, Axl's pet wallaby.

- There are thousands of hours of video footage of the Use Your Illusion world tour in a vault somewhere in Los Angeles. But no one in the band wants to release it. (I wonder why.) Our documentary crew followed us the entire three years, and all this footage was supposed to be made into a full-length documentary. Instead, the footage was never used. It's probably worth millions of dollars and will probably never be seen again. Some of us think that might be a good thing.
- Axl hated singing the same songs every night. I used to say to him that he'd have to play his hit songs forever, and he used to say something along the lines of, "Well, then, shoot me now."
- It seemed that everyone else on tour did, but I never went to the Playboy Mansion. I had so many opportunities to go during my days with Guns N' Roses, but I always thought

I'd go "next time." Well, next time never came, and no one invites me anymore. So sad.

- On Saturday, January 30, 1993, the largest show ever in Australia featured Guns N' Roses at the Eastern Creek Raceway (now the Syndey Motorsport Park) outside of Sydney. We took a helicopter to and from the show because the traffic was so bad—I'm pretty sure there was only one road in, and one road out.

- During our stop in Switzerland, Axl gave me a Jaeger-LeCoultre watch just for the heck of it. He also bought watches for everyone else in his personal entourage that day. I'm guessing that the final bill for the six of us must have been at least $25,000.

- While touring Europe we shared the same private *MGM Grand* plane with Bruce Springsteen and U2. Each band would put bumper stickers with their logo on the outside of the plane.

- Slash, a few members of the band and crew, and I went bowling one night in South America. I met my cousin Bill Baldwin there. He lives in Florida, but he's a pilot for United Airlines and happened to be in South America at the time. So he came out with us that night and we had an amazing time, especially because we were told by the owners of the bowling alley that we could order anything we wanted from the in-house restaurant and a fully stocked bar. There were about fifteen of us there, and we ate and we drank, *a lot*, because they told us we could. For free. So we listened. About five hours later we'd had enough "bowling" and Jack Daniels, so we headed back to the hotel. The next morning I awoke to a knock on my hotel door, and the owner of the bowling alley handed me a bill for about $5,000. I told him I wasn't paying. He told me that I was paying. After arguing for about a half hour, I offered him free tickets to the show, backstage passes, and autographed pictures. I guess it must have been about $5,000 worth of stuff because the bill then magically disappeared.

- Guns N' Roses' album *Use Your Illusion II* sold more than *Use Your Illusion I* during the first week of their release and ever since.

- As most people know, many celebrities do not use their real names when checking into a hotel. Here are a few Guns N' Roses specials:

  Wile E. Coyote
  Dash Riprock
  Colin Sick
  Tung Inmee
  John Shaft
  Hayden Life
  Hugh Jorgan

- Hotels overseas are known for having smaller rooms than we're accustomed to here in the United States—Japan and Europe, especially. I had the pleasure of staying in what I would call the World's Smallest Hotel Room in the amazing Hôtel de Crillon in Paris. The Hôtel de Crillon is one of the most beautiful and most expensive hotels in France, but there is a room in that hotel that stood out in my mind for years, and I had the "pleasure" of staying in it. The elevators in the hotel are tiny as well, but all the rooms (except mine) were normal-sized European rooms. Usually my room was right next door to Axl's Presidential Suite. Unfortunately for me, the only room next to Axl's "big" room was the tiniest room you could ever imagine. It fit a full-sized bed, a tiny dresser, a tinier nightstand, a closet about fourteen inches wide (no, that is not a misprint), and a tiny bathroom. But there was *no*

13-MAY-1992 13:38   FROM TRINIFOLD TRAVEL   TO 0103531617238   P.006/018

TRINIFOLD TRAVEL LTD

WEST END HOUSE
11 HILLS PLACE
LONDON W1R 1AG
Telephone: 071-734-5577 Telex: 396232 HAWKO G
Fax: 071-839-3690
VAT REGISTRATION No. 241 2137 10

TRINIFOLD TRAVEL LIMITED   HOTEL ROOMING LIST

CLIENTS: THE JOHN REESE PARTY

HOTEL: BERKELEY COURT HOTEL, DUBLIN

TAG	GUEST NAME	ROOM TYPE	ROOM NO	DATE IN	DATE OUT
	DASH RIPROCK	PRESIDENTIAL ONE-BEDROOMED SUITE	738	14 MAY	19 MAY
	RICHARD CRANIUM	ONE-BEDROOMED SUITE	542	14 MAY	19 MAY
	JOHN SHAFT	ONE-BEDROOMED SUITE	438	14 MAY	19 MAY
	COLIN SICK	ONE-BEDROOMED SUITE	731	14 MAY	19 MAY
	DOUG GOLDSTEIN	ONE-BEDROOMED SUITE	531	14 MAY	19 MAY
	HUGH JORGAN	KING SINGLE	734	14 MAY	19 MAY
	TUNG INMEE	KING SINGLE	735	14 MAY	19 MAY
	JOHN REESE	KING SINGLE	344	14 MAY	19 MAY
	JERRY GENDRON	KING SINGLE	737	14 MAY	19 MAY
	KIRT KLINGERMAN	KING SINGLE	529	14 MAY	19 MAY
	BILL GREER	KING SINGLE	743	13 MAY	17 MAY
	EARL GABBIDON	KING SINGLE	741	14 MAY	19 MAY
	RON STALNAKER	KING SINGLE	540	14 MAY	19 MAY
	JON ZUCKER	KING SINGLE	729	14 MAY	19 MAY
	BRAD HARPER	KING SINGLE	439	14 MAY	19 MAY
	STEVE THAXTON	KING SINGLE	745	14 MAY	19 MAY
	ROBERT JOHN	KING SINGLE	545	14 MAY	19 MAY
	PAPER KLOG	KING SINGLE	739	14 MAY	19 MAY
	CRAIG DUSWALT	KING SINGLE	736	14 MAY	19 MAY
	AMY BAILEY	KING SINGLE	543	14 MAY	19 MAY
	SABRINA OKAMOTO	KING SINGLE	541	14 MAY	19 MAY
	AUGUST JAKOBSSON	KING SINGLE	539	14 MAY	19 MAY
	LOUIS MARCIANO	KING SINGLE	538	14 MAY	19 MAY
	BOB WEIN	KING SINGLE	536	13 MAY	17 MAY
	JOHN JACKSON (5 PM RELEASE)	KING SINGLE	535	14 MAY	19 MAY
	WENDY LAISTER	KING SINGLE	445	13 MAY	18 MAY
	HUGH FIELDER	KING SINGLE	537	14 MAY	19 MAY
	BERNARD DOHERTY	KING SINGLE	643	14 MAY	17 MAY
	ALEX KOCHAN	KING SINGLE	623	14 MAY	19 MAY
	KAREN KLICHOWSKI	KING SINGLE	625	14 MAY	19 MAY
	TIM FRASER	KING SINGLE	635	14 MAY	19 MAY

3-MAY-92 WED   13:07   671 839 3690   P.06

Typical hotel room list. Notice that six of the first seven names were all aliases. Those were the band members. Axl was Dash Riprock during this leg of the tour. Also notice the name Paper Klog. That was Blake Stanton, Axl's first assistant. He needed an alias as well because it became well known that he was Axl's assistant and fans found out that his room was always next to Axl's. When he left, I got an alias for the same reason. Crazy!

place to walk. The bed took up the whole room, except for the space that was occupied by the doll-sized furniture. I had to walk over the bed to get to the dresser, and back over the bed to get to the bathroom. And I'm claustrophobic. I drank a lot that night just so I could fall asleep.

- On May 26, 1992, at the Berlin Olympic Stadium, built by Adolf Hitler for the 1936 Olympics, a lady had a baby in the audience. From what we heard, they took her to the hospital and everything went great.

- I am a huge Queen fan. I had that in common with Axl and Slash. It was such an incredible honor for me to get to know Brian May, lead guitarist of Queen. Brian opened up for Guns N' Roses for various parts of the tour and it was incredible getting to watch him perform from the side of the stage. Every night I sat there in awe of his talents. Brian loved Guns N' Roses, and he especially loved Axl.

The worst existing picture of me, and Brian May, lead guitarist of Queen. Simply put—Brian May is an amazing guitarist, but even better person.

- One of my favorite Brian May moments happened after the tour. Axl was recording *Chinese Democracy*, and he had asked Brian to lay some guitar tracks down for the new album. Brian was honored. My wife, Natasha, and I were invited to dinner at Axl's that night, with Brian, and we got to hear all the songs they recorded the past few days, before they were ever finished songs.
- During the tour, Gilby Clarke broke his arm riding his motorcycle while we had a few weeks off in Los Angeles. Original rhythm guitarist and songwriter Izzy Stradlin replaced Gilby for a few weeks.
- I had Learjet companies all across America on my "speed dial." Speed dial back then was finding a telephone number in my "Wizard" (electronic phone book) and then finding a pay phone, or using the production phone at the concert. If Axl wanted to go somewhere different than where the band was going, he would get a Learjet. If he wanted to stay at the venue a little longer after the show, and not hold the band up, he would have me rent a Learjet. That is so rock star!
- When we flew on a commercial airline, it was my worst nightmare because getting Axl to the airport was virtually impossible. You think getting him onstage was hard? Ha! I used to have our travel agent book three to four consecutive flights, so that if we missed the first one, we could catch the second one, and if we missed that, we could catch the third one. We would pretty much always miss the first one for sure, and usually get on the second or third flight. Our poor limo driver, Gavin, used to get us from Axl's house in Malibu to LAX in world record time, and somehow he never got a speeding ticket. Thanks, Gavin!

- I carried a pager with me at all times, because believe it or not, cell phones were just coming out and they were originally the size of a Fiat. So I got paged (a lot) and had to find a pay phone. I actually carried a detailed map of easy-to-get-to pay phones all over Los Angeles. It was so much harder back then.

- Saturday, October 3, 1992. Guns N' Roses performed at the Rose Bowl in Pasadena, California. I remember that show very well, and I remember Axl saying after the show, "Now, I feel like I've made it." His goal was always to play at the Rose Bowl. Maybe because of his name, or probably because it is one of the biggest venues we ever played. I vividly remember thinking that day that Axl Rose, for the first time I noticed, seemed extremely proud of his accomplishments. It was the only time I ever saw that in him. We ended up leaving the venue at about 7 a.m. Long night. Great night.

- Axl always wore a bandana. Well, at least 90 percent of the time. His favorite one was red. He had a bunch of red bandanas (backups), but only one favorite. It was worn, and it was soft. He wore his favorite red bandana during concerts, in public, in music videos, and so on. We were very careful to *never* lose that red bandana. But something started happening on the road. After every show we would send Axl's clothes to get dry-cleaned through the hotel's dry-cleaning service. But as I came to find out later, hotels outsource all the dry-cleaning to local stores. After one of the shows we put in the dry-cleaning, and yes, we had his red bandana dry-cleaned. Seems silly now, but we were guys on the road and since we knew nothing about laundry, we just threw all the clothes into the hotel-provided plastic laundry bags (we would need to grab all the bags from the rooms next to ours), call for a bellman to pick the bags up, and it would all come back clean the next day. But the next day came. And when the dry-cleaning arrived, something was missing. The red bandana. Robert and I immediately turned into detectives. We searched the hotel, we went to the dry-cleaning store and searched the premises, and interviewed everyone who worked there. Nothing. But at least we had backup red bandanas. So we pulled one out, and found that it wasn't even close as far as fadedness and wornness. I'm not even sure that those are words, but that's what we thought at the time. So Robert and I went into action. We washed, and dried, and stomped on, and smashed against rocks, two red bandanas to try to get at least one of them to look and feel like Axl's favorite. Apparently it worked, because we laid out his red bandana that night for the show, he put it on and never said a word. It took about ten lost bandanas to figure out that the dry cleaners often knew that Guns N' Roses was staying in the hotel that they worked for, and that it was common practice for dry cleaners across the world to "lose" Axl's red bandana. We finally got smart and just started washing them in a sink after each show. Who knew that Axl's red bandana would be so popular? I know one thing, Axl never knew any of this . . . until now.

- *The Spaghetti Incident?* was a Guns N' Roses album that featured eleven punk cover tunes, the old song "Since I Don't Have You" by the Tokens, and a mystery thirteenth song. I was honored to get a credit in the album liner notes. The thirteenth song is not listed in the liner notes, but if you let the album or CD play through the twelfth song, you will eventually hear the very controversial thirteenth song. It's called "Look at Your Game, Girl." It was written by Charles Manson. To say the band got bad press because of this song is an understatement. But even worse was that the Manson family found out about it and there were death threats on Axl, which meant there were death threats on us because we were at his house every day in between tour dates, and after the tour. There was a two-week period where I feared for my life just showing up for work at Axl's house. I'm not a big believer in guns, but I must say that I was glad that Axl had some guns in his house, just in case. Luckily nothing ever happened, and the death threats and letters from the Manson family just went away after a while. I heard that the song was eventually removed from the newer copies of *The Spaghetti Incident?*.

LAST CONCERT

All things come to an end. But for GNR fans, the end came way too soon. Still, on the final night of the Use Your Illusion tour, I don't think any of us had any idea that things would end so quickly, and so poorly.

THE USE YOUR ILLUSION WORLD TOUR

The Use Your Illusion world tour was the music industry's longest at the time, with 196 shows in thirty-one countries stretching over three calendar years, with grosses around $57 million and at least two riots.

January 20, 1991 — July 17, 1993

Eleven Legs of the Tour

1. Rock in Rio II
2. Warm-up Shows
3. North America & Europe
4. North America & Japan
5. Europe
6. North American Guns N' Roses/Metallica Stadium Tour
7. South America
8. Asia & Oceania
9. North American Skin N' Bones
10. European Skin N' Bones
11. South American Skin N' Bones

1991

January 20 Rio de Janeiro, Brazil, Estadio de Maracanã
January 23 Rio de Janeiro, Brazil, Estadio de Maracanã
May 9 San Francisco, CA, Warfield Theatre
May 11 Los Angeles, CA, Pantages Theatre
May 16 New York, NY, The Ritz
May 24 East Troy, WI, Alpine Valley
May 25 East Troy, WI, Alpine Valley
May 28 Noblesville, IN, Deer Creek Music Theater
May 29 Noblesville, IN, Deer Creek Music Theater
June 1 Grove City, OH, Capital Music Center
June 2 Toledo, OH, Toledo Speedway
June 4 Richfield, OH, Richfield Coliseum
June 5 Richfield, OH, Richfield Coliseum
June 7 Toronto, Ontario, CNE Stadium

June 8 Toronto, Ontario, CNE Stadium

June 10 Saratoga Springs, NY, Performing Arts Center

June 13 Philadelphia, PA, Philadelphia Spectrum

June 17 Uniondale, NY, Nassau Coliseum

June 19 Landover, MD, Capital Centre

June 20 Landover, MD, Capital Centre

June 22 Hampton, VA, Hampton Coliseum

June 23 Charlotte, NC, Charlotte Coliseum

June 25 Greensboro, NC, Greensboro Coliseum

June 26 Knoxville, TN, Thompson-Boling Arena

June 29 Lexington, KY, Rupp Arena

June 30 Birmingham, AL, Birmingham Race Course

July 2 St. Louis, MO, Riverport Performing Arts Center

July 8 Dallas, TX, Starplex Amphitheatre

July 9 Dallas, TX, Starplex Amphitheatre

July 11 Denver, CO, McNichols Sports Arena

July 12 Englewood, CO, Fiddler's Green Amphitheatre

July 13 Salt Lake City, UT, Salt Palace

July 16 Tacoma, WA, Tacoma Dome

July 17 Tacoma, WA, Tacoma Dome

July 19 Mountain View, CA, Shoreline Amphitheater

July 20 Mountain View, CA, Shoreline Amphitheater

July 23 Sacramento, CA, ARCO Arena

July 25 Costa Mesa, CA, Pacific Amphitheater

July 29 Inglewood, CA, Great Western Forum

July 30 Inglewood, CA, Great Western Forum

Aug 2 Inglewood, CA, Great Western Forum

Aug 3 Inglewood, CA, Great Western Forum

Aug 13 Helsinki, Finland, Jäahalli

Aug 14 Helsinki, Finland, Jäahalli

Aug 16 Stockholm, Sweden, Globen

Aug 17 Stockholm, Sweden, Globen

Aug 19 Copenhagen, Denmark, Forum
Aug 24 Mannheim, Germany, Maimarkt-Gelände
Aug 31 London, England, Wembley Stadium
Dec 5 Worcester, MA, Worcester Centrum
Dec 6 Worcester, MA, Worcester Centrum
Dec 9 New York, NY, Madison Square Garden
Dec 10 New York, NY, Madison Square Garden
Dec 13 New York, NY, Madison Square Garden
Dec 16 Philadelphia, PA, Wachovia Spectrum
Dec 17 Philadelphia, PA, Wachovia Spectrum
Dec 28 St. Petersburg, FL, Suncoast Dome
Dec 31 Miami, FL, Joe Robbie Stadium

1992

Jan 3 Baton Rouge, LA, LSU Assembly Centre
Jan 4 Biloxi, MS, Gulf Coast Coliseum
Jan 7 Memphis, TN, The Pyramid
Jan 9 Houston, TX, The Summit
Jan 10 Houston, TX, The Summit
Jan 13 Dayton, OH, Ervin Nutter Center
Jan 14 Dayton, OH, Ervin Nutter Center
Jan 21 Minneapolis, MN, Target Center
Jan 22 Minneapolis, MN, Target Center
Jan 25 Las Vegas, NV, Thomas & Mack Center
Jan 27 San Diego, CA, San Diego Sports Arena
Jan 28 San Diego, CA, San Diego Sports Arena
Jan 31 Chandler, AZ, Compton Terrace
Feb 1 Chandler, AZ, Compton Terrace
Feb 19 Tokyo, Japan, Tokyo Dome
Feb 20 Tokyo, Japan, Tokyo Dome
Feb 22 Tokyo, Japan, Tokyo Dome

Apr 1 Mexico City, Mexico, Sports Palace

Apr 2 Mexico City, Mexico, Sports Palace

Apr 6 Oklahoma City, OK, Myriad Arena

Apr 9 Chicago, IL, Rosemont Horizon

Apr 20 London, England, Wembley Stadium—Freddy Mercury Tribute

May 16 Dublin, Ireland, Slane Castle

May 20 Prague, Czechoslovakia, Strahov Stadium

May 22 Budapest, Hungary, People's Stadium

May 23 Vienna, Austria, Donauinsel Stadium

May 26 Berlin, Germany, Olympic Stadium

May 28 Stuttgart, Germany, Cannstatter Wasen

May 30 Cologne, Germany, Müngersdorfer Stadium

June 3 Hannover, Germany, Niedersachsenstadion

June 6 Paris, France, Hippodrome—Pay-per-view show w/ Aerosmith

June 13 London, England, Wembley Stadium w/ Brian May

June 14 Manchester, England, Maine Road

June 16 Gateshead, England, International Stadium

June 20 Würzburg, Germany, Talavera Mainwiese

June 21 Basel, Switzerland, St. Jakob Stadium

June 23 Rotterdam, Netherlands, Feijenoord Stadion

June 27 Turin, Italy, Stadio Delle Alpi

June 30 Seville, Spain, Estadio Benito Villamarín

July 2 Lisbon, Portugal, Estádio José Alvalade

Guns N' Roses N' Metallica Stadium tour

July 17 Washington, D.C., RFK Stadium

July 18 East Rutherford, NJ, Giants Stadium

July 21 Pontiac, MI, Pontiac Silverdome

July 22 Indianapolis, IN, Hoosier Dome

July 25 Buffalo, NY, Rich Stadium

July 26 Pittsburgh, PA, Three Rivers Stadium

July 29 East Rutherford, NJ, Giants Stadium

Aug 8 Montreal, Quebec, Olympic Stadium—James Hetfield Injured

Aug 25 Phoenix, AZ, Phoenix International Raceway

Aug 27 Las Cruces, NM, Aggie Memorial Stadium

Aug 29 New Orleans, LA, Superdome

Sep 2 Orlando, FL, Citrus Bowl

Sep 4 Houston, TX, Astrodome

Sep 5 Dallas, TX, Texas Stadium

Sep 7 Columbia, SC, Williams-Brice Stadium

Sep 9 Los Angeles, CA, Pauley Pavilion—MTV Awards

Sep 11 Boston, MA, Foxboro Stadium

Sep 13 Toronto, Ontario, Exhibition Stadium

Sep 15 Minneapolis, MN, Metrodome

Sep 17 Kansas City, MO, Arrowhead Stadium

Sep 19 Denver, CO, Mile High Stadium

Sep 24 Oakland, CA, Oakland Coliseum

Sep 27 Los Angeles, CA, Los Angeles Coliseum

Sep 30 San Diego, CA, Jack Murphy Stadium

Oct 3 Pasadena, CA, Rose Bowl

Oct 6 Seattle, WA, Kingdome—I got engaged on October 6, 1992

Nov 25 Caracas, Venezuela, Poliedro de Caracas

Nov 30 Bogotá, Colombia, Estadio El Campín

Dec 2 Santiago, Chile, Estadio Nacional

Dec 5 Buenos Aires, Argentina, River Plate Stadium

Dec 6 Buenos Aires, Argentina, River Plate Stadium

Dec 10 São Paulo, Brazil, Anhembi

Dec 12 São Paulo, Brazil, Anhembi

Dec 13 Rio De Janeiro, Brazil, Autodromo

1993

Jan 12 Tokyo, Japan, Tokyo Dome

Jan 14 Tokyo, Japan, Tokyo Dome

Jan 15 Tokyo, Japan, Tokyo Dome

Jan 30 Sydney, Australia, Eastern Creek Raceway

Feb 1 Melbourne, Australia, Calder Park Raceway

Feb 6 Auckland, New Zealand, Mount Smart Stadium

Feb 23 Austin, TX, Frank Erwin Center

Feb 25 Birmingham, AL, Birmingham-Jefferson Convention Complex

Mar 6 New Haven, CT, New Haven Coliseum

Mar 8 Portland, ME, Cumberland County Civic Center

Mar 9 Hartford, CT, Civic Center

Mar 12 Hamilton, Ontario, Copps Coliseum

Mar 16 Augusta, ME, Augusta Civic Center

Mar 17 Boston, MA, Boston Garden

Mar 20 Iowa City, IA, Carver-Hawkeye Arena

Mar 21 Fargo, ND, Fargo Dome

Mar 24 Winnipeg, Manitoba, Winnipeg Arena

Mar 26 Saskatoon, Saskatchewan, Saskatchewan Place

Mar 28 Edmonton, Alberta, Northlands Coliseum

Mar 30 Vancouver, British Columbia, British Columbia Place

Apr 1 Portland, OR, Portland Coliseum

Apr 3 Sacramento, CA, ARCO Arena

Apr 4 Reno, NV, Lawler Events Arena

Apr 7 Salt Lake City, UT, Delta Center

Apr 9 Rapid City, SD, Rushmore Plaza Civic Center

Apr 10 Omaha, NE, Omaha Civic Auditorium

Apr 13 Detroit, MI, Palace of Auburn Hills

Apr 15 Roanoke, VA, Roanoke Civic Center

Apr 16 Chapel Hill, NC, Dean Smith Center

Apr 21 Guadalajara, Mexico, Estadio Guadalajara
Apr 23 Mexico City, Mexico, Sports Palace
Apr 24 Mexico City, Mexico, Sports Palace
Apr 27 Monterrey, Mexico, Estadio Universitario
Apr 28 Monterrey, Mexico, Estadio Universitario
May 22 Tel Aviv, Israel, Hayarkon Park
May 24 Athens, Greece, Olympic Stadium
May 26 Istanbul, Turkey, İnönü Stadium
May 29 Milton Keynes, England, Milton Keynes Bowl
May 30 Milton Keynes, England, Milton Keynes Bowl
June 2 Vienna, Austria, Praterstadion
June 5 Nijmegen, The Netherlands, Goffertpark
June 6 Nijmegen, The Netherlands, Goffertpark
June 8 Copenhagen, Denmark, Gentofte Stadium
June 10 Oslo, Norway, Valle Hovin
June 12 Stockholm, Sweden, Olympic Stadium
June 16 Basel, Switzerland, St. Jakob
June 18 Bremen, Germany, Weser Stadion
June 19 Cologne, Germany, Müngersdorfer Stadium
June 22 Karlsruhe, Germany, Wildpark Stadium
June 25 Frankfurt, Germany, Wald Stadium
June 26 Munich, Germany, Olympic Stadium
June 29 Modena, Italy, Stadio Alberto Braglia
June 30 Modena, Italy, Stadio Alberto Braglia
July 5 Barcelona, Spain, Olympic Stadium
July 6 Madrid, Spain, Vicente Calderón Stadium
July 8 Nancy, France, Zénith de Nancy
July 9 Lyon, France, Halle Tony Garnier
July 11 Werchter, Belgium, Rock Werchter Festival
July 13 Paris, France, Palais Omnisports de Paris-Bercy
July 16 Buenos Aires, Argentina, River Plate Stadium
July 17 Buenos Aires, Argentina, River Plate Stadium

Axl and a kangaroo. Or wallaby. I still can't tell the difference. Axl loved animals, and somewhere in Australia we went on a private tour of an animal preserve.

Axl and a baby koala bear.

Axl pointing out how dangerous it is for him to dive into a pool of water next to this machine while shooting the Estranged video in Long Beach, CA.

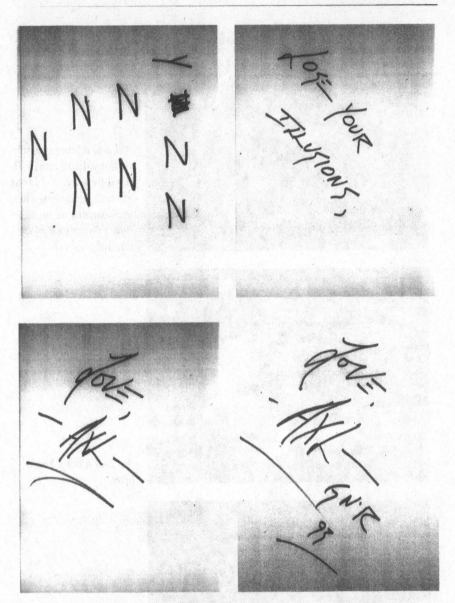

More letters and pages Axl wrote for the "Estranged" video.

BAND TOGETHER

FOUNDATION

A PORTION OF THE PROCEEDS from this book will go to my Band Together Foundation, a foundation designed to help charities and bring about world peace, even if for just one day.

Someday, in the near future, my Band Together Foundation will put on a concert similar to Live Aid. The featured bands will be bands that have broken up for one reason or another. The theory being this—if these bands could put their differences aside for one day to play a concert, maybe we as a world, made up of different nations, could put our differences aside for one day as well, in an effort to bring about world peace.

The Headliner: My dream is to have the original lineup of Guns N' Roses put their differences aside and get back together, even if for only one day, and play a set.

I believe, with all my heart, that they will get back together again. I just have to ask them nicely.

ACKNOWLEDGMENTS

WHEN I STARTED WRITING THIS BOOK I thought it was going to be easy because I was just going to relive a few years from when I toured with Guns N' Roses. But when I really got into it, I realized how detailed I had to be when writing a book like this, and then it got really hard. But I got it done.

What I also realized, as I trudged through memory lane, was that I had a lot of people in my life that I wanted to thank for numerous reasons. This book gives me a chance to do just that. If your name isn't here, I still love you. But I had to narrow it down to people who specifically helped me while I was on tour.

To Robert Street, who discovered me in a small theater in Long Island, New York. Thank you. This is all your fault... and I am truly grateful.

To Russell Hitchcock and Graham Russell of Air Supply, and their manager Barry Siegel. Thank you guys so much for giving me my first opportunity, for showing me the ropes, and for respecting my work even though I was the "assistant." You are truly wonderful friends.

To Chip Forte and Michael Diaz, my buddies from childhood. Thank you for hanging with me and supporting me when this journey started. And thank you both for helping me stay out of trouble by hiding the pieces of our broken beds in the ceiling of the hotel we "destroyed" in Hollywood. They are probably still there. Our little secret.

To Doug Goldstein, thank you for giving me my big break, and for your amazing loyalty throughout the years.

To Axl, thanks for treating me like one of the guys all those years, and thank you for the experience of a lifetime!

To Slash, Duff, Gilby, Dizzy, and Matt, thank you guys for making me feel welcome on the tour, and letting me into your insane world.

To Brain May, thank you for Queen, thank you for keeping in touch, and thank you for putting up with me being a fan.

To Steven Tyler, thanks for the personal concert in your hotel room in Paris, France.

To Teddy Andreadis, Cece Worrall, Anne King, Lisa Maxwell, Roberta Freeman and Tracey Amos, thank you for all the awesome memories on tour. You guys ROCK!

To Robert Finkelstein, thank you for being a great friend all these years, and thank you for helping me stay grounded and sane on the road.

To John Reese, Earl Gabbidon, Steve Thaxton, Sabrina Okamoto, Ron Stalnaker, Robert John, Gene Kirkland, Jerry Gendron, Jon Zucker, Rick "Truck" Beaman, Bill Greer, Bob Wein, Brad Harper, Hans Olin, Tom Maher, Mike Hall, Kirt Klingerman, Chris Jones, Alex Kochan, Dale "Opie" Skjerseth, Tom Mayhue, Mike Mayhue, Adam Day, Will Jennings, Amy Bailey, Stuart Bailey, Blake Stanton, Wendy Laister, August Jakobsson, Tim Fraser, Karen Klichowski, and Louis Marciano, thanks for all your help on the tour, and thanks for being a friend during the good times and the difficult times.

To Beta Lebeis and Del James, thank you for keeping me in the loop all these years.

To the GNR entourage, the GNR documentary team, and the GNR crew, thank you all for the incredible memories.

To the band members of Air Supply—Don Cromwell, Ralph Cooper, Wally Stocker, Ken Rarick, and Frank Esler-Smith (who passed away in 1996), thank you all for your continued friendship, and for letting me play in your awesome world for all those years.

To Steve Rutenbar and Rick Warren. Thank you for your inspiration, and for helping Natasha and I get closer to God, and guiding us (by example) to continue our journey.

To my RockStar MasterMind Members, thank you for helping make my RockStar brand so successful.

To James Malinchak, one of my mentors, thanks for helping me develop the RockStar brand, and for helping me become a successful speaker, author and coach.

To Scott Hoffman and Michael Harriot, my agents, thank you guys for giving me a shot. I think we did great!

To Glenn Yeffeth, my Publisher, and the amazing BenBella team, thank you for putting up with my crazy schedule and my missed deadlines.

To Gary Peterson and Eric Wechter, my editors, thank you for all your hard work in helping me bring this book to fruition.

To Joe Potter, thank you for the great cover design, and for all your design work over the years. You rock!

To Rear Admiral Upper Half Paul Becker, Steve Dantzig, Tom Monahan, Suzanne Forte, Neal Weichel, Marcus Slaton, Dan Westcott, Mark Cole, Ron Medici, Shannon Penrod-Miller, Kevin Kennison, Eric Shapiro, Eric Bauer, Elaine and Ray Parker, Jr., Michael & Ria Cannizzo, Rick & Lori Peters, Steve & Gina Meyer, and Andrew & Cindy Jacquett—thank you all for being my really good friends over the years.

To Larry Broughton, Adam Ace, Bobby Kelly, Maryann Ehmann, Carol Shockley, Rhonda & Phil Vigeant, and Maurice DiMino, thanks for staying with me and inspiring me all these years.

To Glenn Morshower, thank you for becoming one of my closest friends. I love you, brother.

To my wife's family—Tania, Ron, Cameron, Cory, Tricia, Alex and Rashi, thank you for all your love and continued support.

To Pamela, my sister, and her family, William, Courtney, Taylor, Ashley and Michael, I love you all very much. Thank you for all the love you give back.

To Mom and Dad. Thank you for always being there my entire life, through ups and downs, supporting me and encouraging me. And thank you Mom for seeing the future way back in the beginning. It WAS extremely bright. And it gets brighter with every new day. And Dad, thank you for always sticking up for me.

To Natasha, my wife, my best friend, and my soul mate. Thank you for always believing in me. You are the main reason for all my success, and that is why you are "Simply the Best." I love you.

And to Tyler, Ryan and Hayden, my three sons, and the loves of my life. May you be true to who you are, and may you stay as curious, kind, and passionate as you are today, and continue to make great choices. I love you this much, plus infinity.

ABOUT THE AUTHOR

WHEN YOU MEET CRAIG DUSWALT you know he's the real deal and you want to be part of his world. He personifies energy, sincerity, creativity, and just plain old fun.

Craig's background with Guns N' Roses and Air Supply gives you the secret insight into his formula for success. Their diverse styles of music offer a great metaphor to help identify what makes him so unique, yet so effective. His style is strong, yet adaptive; he is patient, yet demanding; he is high energy, yet focused. Just like the rock bands of his past, Craig leads clients on a journey of discovery, discipline, hard work, creative explosion, and massive delivery of consistent results.

He has found the unique balance between building on the lessons of his past and bringing them to life in his own business through the RockStar brand he delivers to clients through his speaking, his writing, and his coaching. Craig believes in out-of-the-box thinking to break through barriers of traditional marketing and focuses on ways to stand out from the competition.

Craig believes that everyone can be a RockStar in their industry and he is living proof that his methods work.